Beyond Your Bubble

Through my years moderating healthy conversations between conservatives and progressives, I deeply believe that the practical skills in *Beyond Your Bubble* will breathe new life into our democracy.

—J. CHRISTOPHER COLLINS, FOUNDER,
DIFFERENT TOGETHER

In a gentle and compassionate way, the author reminds us of things we know, but easily forget, when we care deeply about an issue.

—DON DAVIS, PHD, COAUTHOR OF CULTURAL HUMILITY:
ENGAGING DIVERSE IDENTITIES IN THERAPY,
GEORGIA STATE UNIVERSITY, ATLANTA

dialogue:
interchange and discussion of ideas, esp. when open and frank,
as in seeking mutual understanding or harmony

—Collins Dictionary

Skills and Strategies for Conversations That Work

Beyond Your Bubble

HOW TO CONNECT ACROSS THE POLITICAL DIVIDE

TANIA ISRAEL, PHD

 AMERICAN PSYCHOLOGICAL ASSOCIATION

Published by
American Psychological Association
750 First Street, NE
Washington, DC 20002
https://www.apa.org

Order Department
https://www.apa.org/pubs/books
order@apa.org

In the U.K., Europe, Africa, and the Middle East, copies may be ordered from
Eurospan
https://www.eurospanbookstore.com/apa
info@eurospangroup.com

Typeset in Sabon by Circle Graphics, Inc., Reisterstown, MD

Printer: Sheridan Books, Chelsea, MI
Cover Designer: Melissa Jane Barrett, Provo, UT

Library of Congress Cataloging-in-Publication Data

Names: Israel, Tania, author.
Title: Beyond your bubble : how to connect across the political divide, skills and strategies for conversations that work / Tania Israel.
Description: Washington : American Psychological Association, 2020. | Includes bibliographical references and index.
Identifiers: LCCN 2020013879 (print) | LCCN 2020013880 (ebook) | ISBN 9781433833557 (paperback) | ISBN 9781433833687 (ebook)
Subjects: LCSH: Communication—Psychological aspects. | Public speaking—Psychological aspects. | Communication in politics—Psychological aspects.
Classification: LCC BF637.C45 I77 2021 (print) | LCC BF637.C45 (ebook) | DDC 153.6—dc23
LC record available at https://lccn.loc.gov/2020013879
LC ebook record available at https://lccn.loc.gov/2020013880

https://doi.org/10.1037/0000202-000

CONTENTS

ACTIVITIES YOU CAN DO ON YOUR OWN

ACKNOWLEDGMENTS

This book was developed in conversation and community. To the neighbors, community leaders, faith congregants, and activists who participated in my workshops, I am so grateful. Your experiences, comments, and questions shaped my understanding of what's needed for dialogue to work. I also want to thank every person who talked with me about this topic. Family, friends, and acquaintances who expressed interest in the book, shared your thoughts, and reminded me of the value of this work, I appreciate you. Special thanks to David Landecker, who was always game to engage in conversations that deepened my thinking and helped me to articulate my ideas.

This book would not exist without my amazing writing companions. My work wife and writing buddy, Laury Oaks, whose wisdom, support, and good will have helped me persist on this project and in all of my professional roles. Gabriela Soto Laveaga, who Pomodoroed with me from across the country at ridiculous hours and through weekend marathons to help me crank out drafts of the manuscript. And my dear friend and Story Charmer, Pema Rocker, whose coaching, editing, reviewing, and writing company brought this book into being, from the initial envisioning to the final copyedit. How fortunate I am to have all of you in my corner.

Several graduate students assisted at various points in the development of this project: Krishna Kary collaborated on the original concept for the flowchart, Sam del Castillo compiled workshop feedback, and Kristina Esopo tracked down references and other details. Many thanks to you for your thoughtful contributions. Thanks to everyone at APA Books, who helped bring this project to fruition, especially Chris Kelaher, who pursued me relentlessly, and Tyler Aune, who offered me insightful feedback, guidance, and patience.

Finally, I want to acknowledge the United States of America. Our differences are woven into the fabric of our country; our ability to connect across these differences strengthens us collectively. I feel so fortunate to be part of this amazing mix of people. My aspiration is that this book cultivates our compassion and skills to help us reach our greatest potential.

Beyond
Your
Bubble

INTRODUCTION:
THE STATE OF OUR UNION

The United States is acutely divided. We are #metoo, and we are "Make America great again." We are gun rights, and we are gun control. We are oil and coal, and we are climate change. We are tearing down Confederate monuments, and we are building walls to keep immigrants out. We are marching and shouting, and we are weeping and cheering. We are tweeting and sharing, and we are liking and unfriending. We are in turmoil.

Political polarization is at an all-time high, and it's affecting us. Democrats and Republicans hold more disparate views on issues and more negative views of each other than ever before in recent history.[1] This conflict causes gridlock in Washington, DC, but it also has an impact closer to home. You might have a childhood friend whose Facebook posts upset you. You might avoid family gatherings. You might distance yourself from friends. You might feel tense about interacting with certain coworkers. This divisiveness is taking a toll on the mental health of the American public, with most adults reporting increased stress associated with political conflict.[2]

We are having trouble talking with and listening to people whose political views are different from our own. We choose news

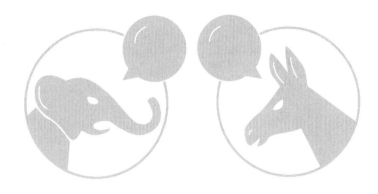

sources that support our beliefs. Our choices guide the complex algorithms of social media that tell us what we want to hear and shield us from opposing views. We find ourselves in a collective existential crisis as we disagree about what is truth. As media frames opposing viewpoints as shouting matches and comments on Facebook and Twitter convey vitriol and accusation, we shy away from people and organizations whose positions may conflict with our own. We take refuge in echo chambers of like-minded people expressing views we support, cheering each other on as we rake our common enemies over the coals. Within our bubbles, we are free from challenge, safe from alternative perspectives, comforted by our own certainty.

Made of soap and water, bubbles are beautiful and fun and magical, but they are also fragile. The bubbles we create from political insulation are similarly unsustainable. If we cannot survive outside of our bubbles; if we cannot tolerate listening to our friends and families and neighbors; if we cannot see beyond our own perspectives; if we view our fellow citizens as enemies, how can we sustain our relationships, our communities, our country?

MOVING BEYOND OUR BUBBLES

Despite these divisive dynamics, I am hopeful we can bridge the political divide. My personal and professional experiences inform this hope. As a professor of counseling psychology, I teach classes on helping skills, leadership, and community collaboration. I conduct research that informs policy and practice, and my expertise has been solicited by the Institute of Medicine, Congress, and the White House. I've organized and facilitated educational programs and difficult dialogues in communities and professional settings about a range of topics including sexual orientation, law enforcement, and religion. My life's work is not just about understanding problems; it's about what can be done to alleviate them.

In the wake of the 2016 election, the problem of political polarization was evident, and I started developing tools to help people who were struggling with the disconnect between themselves and people outside their bubble. "The Flowchart That Will Resolve All Political Conflict in Our Country," which I introduce in Chapter 1, is where I began. Within 6 months after the election, I was offering a 2-hour interactive, skills-building workshop for my local community. Hundreds of people have participated in the program since that time, with an overwhelmingly positive response.

When I ask people what they're taking away from the workshop, participants say they have developed a more open mind, greater willingness to listen to others, less fear of confrontation, and confidence to keep trying to connect rather than withdraw. They also express commitments to use the skills and perspectives they gained. For example, one participant said, "I need to stop trying to convince others on the 'other side' of their erroneous thinking, and instead listen more to understand where they are coming from. " One described the workshop as "a reminder that to have true dialogue, I must listen and be open, even when the ideas presented feel threatening." Another stated, "I will try to judge less, take my time, and look at other people's views." Particularly promising was the shift from feeling discouraged to the expression of hope.

People started asking me for more resources—more than I could offer in a flowchart or 2-hour session—so I wrote this book. My aim is to support people who want to connect with those who have different political views and values by offering concrete skills, as well as overarching principles and strategies that will promote constructive conversation. Moreover, as a psychologist, I am aware of the vast knowledge base my field can offer to address challenges people are facing due to political polarization, and I want to make these resources available to everyone.

Many people feel paralyzed by political polarization. I encounter a lot of pessimism that such dialogue is a viable or desirable endeavor. On the basis of my experience in these workshops, I am optimistic about the potential to bridge the political divide through dialogue. *Beyond Your Bubble* offers teachable skills and information that can move us toward civility and connection. I am hopeful, and, equipped with the tools herein, I believe you will be, too.

Although this book is based primarily on experiences within the United States, conflict and desire for dialogue exist throughout the world. One only need look at the United Kingdom,[3] Brazil,[4] and Malaysia[5] to realize that polarization and opportunities for bridging the divide are widespread. The political divisions and contentious issues that keep people from dialogue may vary across the globe, and it is important to consider cultural values and communication to guide implementation of these strategies in varying contexts. Nonetheless, I suspect there are ideas and guidance in this book that will be useful around the world.

MY EXPERIENCE WITH DIALOGUE

As you may have sensed, I don't shy away from controversial subjects. In fact, one of my most meaningful dialogue experiences focused on a highly divisive topic. I've been pro-choice since high school, a view that became further solidified as I became a women's studies major and worked as a pregnancy counselor after college. My job was at a clinic that provided reproductive health care, including abortions; I counseled hundreds of women with unintended pregnancies, providing contraceptive education and support. Regularly, I steeled myself to hurry past protesters on my way into work. As they hurled accusations of "baby killer" toward me, the last thing I wanted to do was prolong my interactions with pro-life advocates. I had come to see pro-lifers as antiwoman and hypocritical, as I witnessed how they distressed our patients.

Over time, however, I grew weary of the animosity I felt toward the pro-lifers. And I recognized that my anger was not benefiting the women I was trying to help. Thanks to a timely radio story, I learned about Common Ground,[6] a St. Louis–based group that was fostering dialogue among pro-choice and pro-life individuals. I reached out to the director of a local pro-life crisis pregnancy center to start a Common Ground group in our town. She was game, and we invited our respective communities to participate. Despite some skepticism and resistance from my fellow pro-choice advocates, several welcomed the opportunity to talk with pro-lifers. Three years earlier, when I started work at the clinic, I certainly would not have imagined myself reaching out to collaborate with the director of a pro-life crisis pregnancy center to start a dialogue group. Yet there I was, at the public library in Charlottesville, Virginia, with pro-life and pro-choice people who wanted to talk with and listen to each other.

At the meetings, we established ground rules, shared our perspectives, and identified areas of agreement. For me, these conversations humanized people whose views I was in the habit of dismissing as ignorant. Hearing them describe their values, I recognized a logic and morality that, although different from my own, were consistent with their beliefs and experiences. Evaluated from my frame of reference, their stance didn't make sense; however, the underlying stories revealed new insights that guided me to understand how they arrived at their conclusions. It became clear that the opinions about abortion voiced in this group were far more complex than could be represented on bumper stickers and that the usual spokespeople for the opposing sides did not represent the range of individuals who identified with these labels. I listened to a wide array of people, including pro-life feminists and pro-choice people of faith. I found myself articulating my own values with greater nuance than I typically had occasion to express within pro-choice circles (where everyone presumably has a similar viewpoint). This dialogue did not change my views on reproductive choice, but it did change my views about people who disagree with me on abortion. While still recognizing our differences, it had become clear to me that we were all ethical, intelligent, good-hearted people. Best of all, my participation in Common Ground showed me how dialogue could provide insight into the healing process within conflicted communities. We might not end up agreeing on substantive policy or values, but we could humanize rather than demonize those with whom we disagree, we could exchange ideas respectfully, we could deepen our understanding of ourselves and each other. Given the internal and external turmoil I had experienced regarding pro-life advocates, these felt like very satisfying outcomes.

Flash forward 2 decades: After the 2016 election, I saw liberals struggling to understand how so many people could vote for Donald Trump. I heard conservatives feeling threatened and silenced by social justice advocates. I witnessed accusations of stupidity and corruption hurled from both sides. I worried that our deep divisions were unraveling our democracy. I sought out resources, and I found some experts saying we need to talk to each other, but it was harder to find guidance on how to do so. As someone who is engaged in community and in politics, who teaches people how to heal, and who has experienced the power of dialogue, I thought I might have something to contribute. This book is my offering to the state of our union and to all of you.

MEET KEVIN AND CELINE[7]

Celine has an associate's degree and is an office manager in a small business. She and her friends care a lot about their local community. She supports her church and is active in her kids' school. She considers herself pro-life, but she's not an activist. Celine feels like liberals are always criticizing people like her, putting them down, calling them uneducated, so she mostly limits conversations with people who disagree about politics.

Kevin works for a nonprofit. He donates money to political organizations and is mystified by people who watch Fox News. He feels a sense of urgency about climate change and is incensed by rollbacks on environmental regulation. He hasn't been to church since he left home for college 20 years ago. He embraces opportunities to advocate for social justice.

Kevin and Celine are cousins. They've been avoiding each other because their opposing politics have gotten them into trouble at holiday gatherings and on Facebook in recent years. But their kids miss each other, so when they saw *Beyond Your Bubble* on Instagram, they got this book for their parents. Knowing they'd all see each other at an upcoming family wedding, the teens suggested their parents might each read it to help get past their differences. Celine and Kevin agreed, and they broke the ice at the wedding by making a plan to meet up and dialogue the following week.

We'll be following Celine and Kevin throughout the book as they engage in dialogue with each other. You'll see how they use the skills and activities to connect across political difference.

HOW TO USE THIS BOOK

Beyond Your Bubble is intended as a resource for people who are interested in engaging in dialogue across political lines. It won't simply tell you what you should do; it will help you develop the skills to do it. Plus, the content is backed by scientific evidence and a wide range of human experience to give you practical and well-supported guidance on what fosters connection and understanding. This makes your new dialogue skills useful regardless of your place on the political spectrum and for deepening your conversations in any relationship and circumstance. You may be skeptical of dialogue, and you may encounter others who are disinclined to connect across the political divide. This book will help you decide whether you want to have dialogue, with whom, and in what contexts.

Read the book on your own or with other people who are interested in practicing these skills, such as an interactive book club. Reading the book with others may deepen your experience and better prepare you for dialogue. Alternatively, working through it alone might give you an opportunity to reflect on the material before trying to apply it. Either way, you will be exposed to useful ideas and skills.

Whether or not you read the book with others, practicing the skills you learn here will be helpful. You will get better at them and feel more confident, which will also increase your likelihood of engaging in meaningful dialogue on political themes. Whether you're someone who dives right into weighty political conflict or shies away from discord, you'll find something in this book that will help you to be more effective interacting with folks across the political divide.

Chapter 1 will give you a sense of what dialogue is and what it isn't. It will also help you identify what draws you to dialogue and what gets in the way. You will learn that a successful exchange can be boiled down to just two things, and the rest of the book should equip you to do these two things well.

Is it hard to even imagine where to start? If so, Chapter 2 will lay the groundwork. You'll engage in individual preparation, as well as gain ideas for how to initiate dialogue.

Chapter 3 is about listening: why it's important and how to listen effectively using nonverbal signals, paraphrasing, and questions. If you have a difficult time responding without arguing, this will be a great chapter for you.

If you feel your blood pressure rising just imagining talking with someone on the other side of the political divide, Chapter 4 will help you anticipate and manage feelings that arise so you can keep your cool and stay engaged.

Chapter 5 offers strategies for seeing things through another person's eyes. If you find yourself wondering, "How could someone possibly think that?" try a perspective-shifting activity and learn different ways of viewing moral values.

Want to learn how to share your views most effectively? Chapter 6 explains how to tell your story, find common ground, and be as persuasive as possible. In my experience, how to talk is one of the first things people want to focus on. If you're eager to get to this material, it's fine to start there, but I encourage you to go back to familiarize yourself with Chapters 2 through 5. Talking is not very effective without the foundation of the other skills.

Chapter 7 puts dialogue skills in context. How will dialogue be affected by the relationship between you and another person, the skill level of both parties, the origins of your values.

How can sharing a pizza illustrate dynamics of dialogue across political lines?

Chapter 8 will help you develop an action plan and other tools to prepare for a successful conversation, including how to bring your dialogue to a close. You'll also find some final thoughts and encouragement to prepare you for dialogue. After that, all that's left to do is use the skills you've learned!

Additional materials will help you hone and implement your dialogue skills. If the book whets your appetite to read more or find groups supporting dialogue, check out the Additional Resources. The Communication Guidelines can help lay the groundwork for successful dialogue. If you're reading the book with others and want to practice skills, you'll find instructions for activities in Activities to Try With a Partner.

You might choose to read the book from cover to cover, or you might focus on skills that are most challenging for you. It might be helpful to skim the entire book, then dig deeper into areas that contain stumbling blocks for you.

I offer a caveat that this book is about applying these skills within the context of dialogue across political lines. It does not necessarily apply to the way you communicate with people who agree with you. Nor should these principles be assumed to apply to rhetoric in speeches or in written materials. There are other resources that address how to frame an argument to appeal to liberals and conservatives (for example, *Don't Think of an Elephant*[8] and other works by George Lakoff, as well as research studies on moral framing[9]). There is a body of literature on persuasion outside of an interpersonal context (e.g., media messages) and for the purposes of marketing. Much of this literature focuses more on the content of the message than on the interpersonal context in which the message is delivered. That said, I think you will find material in this book that will inform your understanding of and ability to communicate with people across the range of political positions.

As you embark on this journey, I want to say how encouraged I am by your interest and your willingness to try to reach across the political divide. Openness to dialogue and to diverse viewpoints are important qualities as we work toward unifying our country and our world. Thank you for joining me in this brave endeavor.

NOTES

1. Pew Research Center. (2017). *The partisan divide on political values grows even wider.* https://www.people-press.org/2017/10/05/the-partisan-divide-on-political-values-grows-even-wider/
2. American Psychological Association. (2017). *Stress in America: The state of our nation.* https://www.apa.org/news/press/releases/stress/2017/state-nation.pdf
3. Ford, R., & Goodwin, M. (2017). Britain after Brexit: A nation divided. *Journal of Democracy, 28,* 17–30.
4. Ortellado, P., & Ribeiro, M. M. (2018, August 3). Mapping Brazil's political polarization online. *The Conversation.* https://theconversation.com/mapping-brazils-political-polarization-online-96434
5. Bonura, C. (2015). *Political polarization, transition, and civil society in Thailand and Malaysia.* Middle East Institute. https://www.mei.edu/publications/political-polarization-transition-and-civil-society-thailand-and-malaysia
6. Kelly, J. R. (1996). Truth, not truce: "Common Ground" on abortion, a movement within both movements. In J. L. Nolan (Ed.), *The American culture wars: Current contests and future prospects* (pp. 213–242). University Press of Virginia.
7. These characters are fictitious. No identification with actual persons (living or deceased) is intended or should be inferred.
8. Lakoff, G. (2014). *The all new, don't think of an elephant! Know your values and frame the debate.* Chelsea Green.
9. Feinberg, M., & Willer, R. (2015). From gulf to bridge: When do moral arguments facilitate political influence? *Personality and Social Psychology Bulletin, 41*(12), 1665–1681. https://doi.org/10.1177/0146167215607842

CHAPTER 1

GETTING STARTED: THE BASICS OF MEANINGFUL DIALOGUE

Facing the chasm of political discord, you may feel frustrated, angry, motivated, discouraged, hopeless, energized, exhausted, and more. How do you deal with these feelings? What actions do you take? Do you write to your elected representatives to advocate for policy in line with your views? Do you post on social media? Do you organize with others from your side to take local action? Do you unfriend people on Facebook who post opposing viewpoints? Do you burn out and start avoiding the news? Perhaps you simply go about your life trying to avoid interpersonal land mines. With all of these options available, why is dialogue—conversation with those on the other side—a worthwhile activity? How might it complement or replace these other options?

Political divisiveness is challenging because of both the external conflict and the ways it can stir up people's internal emotional state. Although you may view conversations with folks on the other side as a source of tension, if approached skillfully, they can be a route to healing. We live in interpersonal contexts—in family, community, country. When these contexts are defined by discord, we sacrifice one of the most important resources we have: human connection. Dialogue offers a means to navigate our way out of conflict.

Dialogue also offers the possibility of change, of shifting understandings and ideas and relationships. Conversation foments discovery. We can figure things out and learn through conversation. There are numerous reasons to have dialogue; the specific motivations differ depending on individuals and their circumstances. Later in this chapter, you'll have an opportunity to reflect on your own reasons, as well as potential obstacles. But first, let's consider what dialogue is and isn't.

WHAT KIND OF CONVERSATION ARE WE TALKING ABOUT?

When you imagine communication across political lines, what comes to mind? Shouting matches? Twitter wars? Uncomfortable silences? For many, contemporary communication platforms (such as social media) and a newly emerged culture of contentious, continuously consumed politics, seed a narrow perception of political dialogue and how individuals engage in it. This book will help you envision and engage in productive conversations with people whose views and values differ from your own. *Dialogue* is the term I use for these conversations. You might have a different way of thinking about it, but try to consider the following parameters, whatever you actually call it.

First, I'll be describing how to have a conversation that takes place face to face, not Facebook to Facebook. Our communication on social media tends to focus on the expression of one's own views, without trying to comprehend other people's positions. This may feel satisfying in the short term, but it does not promote mutual understanding and connection. It does not promote dialogue.

Second, by "across political lines," I mean someone whose views or values differ from your own. You might want to have dialogue with someone who is diametrically opposed to you politically, but the skills in this book will also be helpful in conversation with someone who does not necessarily hold the most extreme views on "the other side." Sometimes when we imagine ourselves in discussion with a person who disagrees with us politically, we have in our minds that we are going to be debating the spokespeople for what we disagree with. When we imagine talking with the people we see on TV or hear on the radio, we think of individuals who are identified representatives for these views, whose role it is to express these views in pure or simplified terms. What's imperative to remember is that the media represent a limited range of viewpoints. In reality, there are many viewpoints between the extremes, and dialogue can reveal these nuanced and varied perspectives.

This book also focuses on dialogue with someone who *wants* to be in dialogue. This piece is crucial because I hear people say sometimes, "Well, how am I supposed to dialogue if the other person doesn't want to?" We'll be more productive if we start with the low-hanging fruit. Let's consider how we get ourselves to a place where we're willing and feel prepared to engage in dialogue with a partner who is also willing to do so.

Finally, I want to point out that just because you *can* have dialogue doesn't mean you *must* in every situation. It's an opportunity, not a mandate. I'm not going to say, "You've got to get out there and have dialogue because now you know how." You get to make choices about whether to participate in dialogue.

Speaking of choices, you're going to make a lot of choices within a dialogue. To help visualize these choices, I created a resource that I jokingly refer to as "The Flowchart That Will Resolve All Political Conflict in Our Country" (or, as a friend commented, "way to overpromise!"; see Figure 1.1). This diagram will give you a sense of the choices you get to make along the way; about whether you want to have dialogue and, if so, how you want to do it. It will help you be aware of your options, so you can have *conscious* conversations.

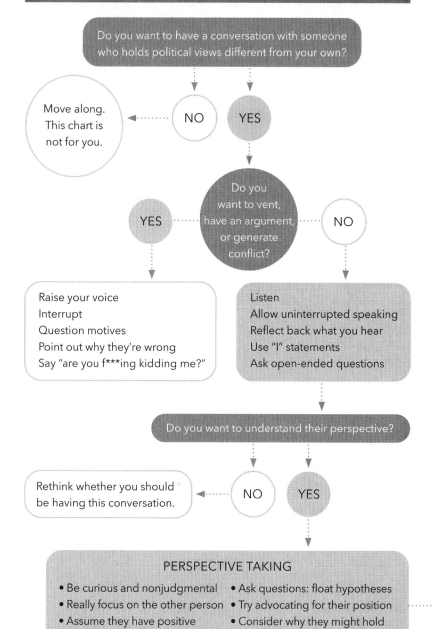

FIGURE 1.1. The Flowchart That Will Resolve All Political Conflict in Our Country

Do you want to have a conversation with someone who holds political views different from your own?

NO → Move along. This chart is not for you.

YES

Do you want to vent, have an argument, or generate conflict?

YES:
Raise your voice
Interrupt
Question motives
Point out why they're wrong
Say "are you f***ing kidding me?"

NO:
Listen
Allow uninterrupted speaking
Reflect back what you hear
Use "I" statements
Ask open-ended questions

Do you want to understand their perspective?

NO → Rethink whether you should be having this conversation.

YES

PERSPECTIVE TAKING
• Be curious and nonjudgmental
• Really focus on the other person
• Assume they have positive intentions
• Ask questions: float hypotheses
• Try advocating for their position
• Consider why they might hold their views

What is your goal?

PERSUADE

Do you understand their perspective? Can you treat them with respect? If not, go back to listening and perspective taking. If so, and if you still want to try to persuade them, carry on . . .

COMMON GROUND

Seek shared personal or political hopes, fears, goals, interests, likes, dislikes, experiences. Agree to disagree.

Liberals and Conservatives all have morals, but they have different priorities. Where are they on the political spectrum?

LEFT

Appeal to:
- Sympathy
- Compassion
- Nurturance
- Rights
- Justice

RIGHT

Appeal to:
- Loyalty
- Obligations
- Authority/respect
- Traditions
- Social order
- Purity/sanctity

HOW CAN I DEAL WITH DISTRESSING FEELINGS THAT COME UP DURING DIALOGUE?

- Anticipate and be aware of reactions
- Breathe
- Remember your motivations
- Pause the dialogue
- Seek support elsewhere

DIALOGUE, DISCOURSE, AND DEBATE

To help envision what kind of conversation we're talking about, let's take a moment to distinguish dialogue from some other forms of communication: diatribe, discourse, and debate. The definitions presented here are not universal, but they may help you get a sense of the type of dialogue this book advocates.

First, we are not talking about *diatribe*. This is not about listening to your neighbor spew vitriol, nor is it about you spewing vitriol at your neighbor. Venting can have an important role in expressing frustration and seeking support and validation; however, this is most productively accomplished with people who hold similar views to your own.

In *debate*, the goal is to win—and not even necessarily from a perspective you agree with. Rather, it's about crafting an argument in such a way that you logically win the point. Debate is about conquering an opponent in the eyes of outside evaluators. It's not about the relationship between people on opposing sides of an issue.

Discourse refers to a sharing of ideas, and civil discourse is about being able to share ideas back and forth without hostility. Discourse can be a useful exercise in articulating and introducing ideas. The limitation is that, if the ideas are shared without context to understand the values and experiences of the people who hold them, discourse does not necessarily deepen understanding or connection.

Dialogue, in contrast, is about sharing ideas, but it goes deeper than that. It's about being able to understand ideas and the people who hold them—and being able to make a connection with these people. Because it is based in human connection, dialogue can go beyond debate and discourse by helping people feel connected even when they disagree. It can help people understand different views within the context of the values and experiences from which they arise.

I hear *diatribe, discourse,* and *debate* everywhere. I also hear frustration with the outcomes—they don't move the conversation forward, they rupture relationships, and they are exhausting. The ineffectiveness of these approaches leads people to seek alternatives. Maybe it's the reason you are reading this book. People might think that debate or discourse will solve the problem, but dialogue is what we need.

WHAT INSPIRES OR INTERFERES WITH DIALOGUE?

There's something wonderful about you: You want to know more about dialogue, you want to connect with people who come from a different political perspective. Something has drawn you to this topic, to this book. But perhaps conversation across political lines hasn't always gone well, or maybe it hasn't happened at all. Something gets in the way. Most of us who have an interest in this topic can identify motivations to engage in dialogue, as well as barriers that interfere with our success. This section will help you reflect on yours.

Motivations for Dialogue

Why are you interested in dialogue across political lines? Your motivation to engage in such conversations is key to the process ahead. Clarity about why you want to do this will help move you toward rather than avoid conversation, focus the content and approach to dialogue, and remind you to stay engaged when you might want to leave.

Take a moment to consider: Do any of the following describe what you hope to gain from such dialogue?

- There's someone in my life with whom I want to maintain a good relationship.

- I want to persuade or convince others to see things the way I do.
- I'm having trouble understanding why people think the way they do.
- I'm hoping we can find common ground.
- I'm feeling distressed about political conflict.
- I want to help heal the political divide.
- Some other reason (what is it?)

Maybe you identified that you are seeking a way to maintain a good relationship with someone in your life. Did your aunt, who remembers every birthday and always celebrates your successes, vote for someone who makes your skin crawl? Perhaps you find yourself avoiding her calls and keeping your distance at family gatherings. Maybe the people in your work environment are slanted toward the other side of the political spectrum from you, and it stresses you out every time they break into cavalier or insensitive banter about it. In these cases, you might feel unskilled at how to have productive dialogue with people you know. Alternatively, you might not have people in your circle whose views contrast with your own, in which case you might not have a specific person in mind but rather have a general desire to reach out to people with different views.

You might hope to accomplish a variety of goals through dialogue. For example, maybe you're thinking that gridlock among politicians is not moving things forward, but you're hopeful that dialogue can help find solutions to problems in your community or society. Or what if you're concerned that others haven't been exposed to information you're aware of, and you want to share research or beliefs or experiences to encourage them to support your positions? You might think, "If they only knew. . . ." Perhaps you have trouble understanding why people think or behave as they do, and you feel like your views are misunderstood by people on "the other side." Thus, you might hope dialogue can create mutual understanding: You can understand them better, and they can understand your perspective.

As one person told me, "All I have to do is turn on the radio or the TV, and I find my blood pressure rising. I don't want to be triggered all the time." Others feel trapped in situations with someone whose views differ from their own—on an airplane with a stranger, in a car with a supervisor, at a dinner party. These situations, even the anticipation of them, cause stress. You may relate and want to know how to deal with it.

Many of us seek dialogue for personal reasons related to our own lives. Some may also have deeper, more global motivations to help heal the political divide. In faith communities, I find shared values to motivate dialogue, such as Christianity's maxim "love thy neighbor," Buddhism's practice of compassion, and Judaism's *tikkun olam*, which encourages us to heal what is broken in the world.

You may desire a specific dialogue with a fairly limited outcome, such as making peace with your cousin in advance of Thanksgiving dinner. Alternatively, your motivation may be broader—not only to have a dialogue but also to be someone who engages in dialogue, to deepen your skill set to enable you to reach across political lines when you happen to encounter people on "the other side," or even to cultivate such opportunities. Whether your goals for dialogue are long term or more narrowly defined, you can harness your motivations to support your efforts.

Barriers to Dialogue

Despite the many varied motivations for engaging in dialogue across political lines, the dearth of dialogue shows that something must be standing in the way. I'm guessing that as many motivations as you have for wanting dialogue, you might also struggle against common, or even not-so-common, barriers. Either way, they keep you from engaging across political lines. Do any of these barriers resonate for you?

- Anger (my own)
- Anger (another person's)
- Polarization that feels insurmountable
- Lack of shared information
- Feelings of vulnerability
- Avoidance of conflict
- Lack of interest in understanding opposing views
- Belief it's a zero-sum game
- Fear of being forced into dialogue and allowing an attack on deeply held beliefs

Anger is one of the most prominent barriers, and it has several dimensions. First is a fear of getting angry and, once incensed, being unable to engage in productive conversation. As one person told me, "Blowing my top is not the goal of dialogue." You may feel angry at a specific person you know, or you may be angry about groups of people who hold a particular view or who behave or vote in a certain way. You may be anticipating anger based on feelings that have arisen in past conversations, or on the news or social media.

Anger may also be a barrier to dialogue when you anticipate that the other person will be angry. You may have heard this particular person get angry in the past, or you may imagine they will be angry due to the tone of people who publicly support similar positions. Media representation of political discussions gives us reason to think anger is an inevitable aspect of the conversation. Engaging with someone who is angry can make you feel uncomfortable, threatened, and vulnerable. If you feel helpless and unable to diffuse the anger, you may think that such encounters don't do anyone any good. Imagining anger directed at you may make you shy away from dialogue.

Perhaps you feel hopeless about connecting with people across the divide. You perceive political polarization as a chasm too wide to bridge. Their experiences are too different from your own, their values too extreme, their beliefs too biased. How can we possibly find common ground?

Given the disparate lenses of various news sources and social media echo chambers these days, basic agreement on factual information is challenging. People tell me they don't know how to talk to others who hold certain beliefs. They feel frustrated that they can't argue against information they perceive to be false, because, generally, people will believe whatever information they're exposed to—even if it's not correct. You may feel like folks on the other side believe what they do because of misinformation, although you notice that your attempts to correct this misinformation shut down dialogue.

Do you believe people on the other side of the political divide even *want* to engage in dialogue? When I am asked if people from both sides really attend my workshops. I sense skepticism behind this question. I find the underlying sentiment is, "Why should I listen to *them* if they're not going to listen to *me*?"

The simple answer: Mistrust of the other side may be based in distorted and limited understanding (see Chapter 5 for an in-depth look into this). Both sides may be making assumptions about each other based on visible attributes, group identities, manner of speech, or other characteristics. Becoming more conscious about your assumptions will help you to have a clearer view of people and to engage in meaningful dialogue that can enable deeper understanding. Lack of contact with and distorted views of people across the political divide also make it difficult to trust that someone on the other side could engage in good faith, and this mistrust interferes with dialogue.

Exposing yourself to views that contrast with your own may bring up feelings of vulnerability. Some people describe this vulnerability as fear: of feeling attacked, of losing power, of losing certainty, of feeling unsupported and challenged. If someone holds views about a group of people you belong to, you may feel misunderstood, misrepresented, dismissed, or degraded. And you may want to protect yourself from these feelings by avoiding dialogue or by keeping yourself emotionally removed by debating rather than dialoguing. You may find yourself using speech as a shield against these feelings of vulnerability, but you will need to lower the shield and risk feeling vulnerable for dialogue to work.

You might notice that you've been avoiding discussing political issues with people in your life who hold differing views because you're concerned about causing conflict in these relationships. You might be worried about losing a friend or losing a connection with a relative you've always felt close to. You might be concerned about lacking solidarity with those on "your side." Engaging in dialogue with someone who disagrees may be seen as a betrayal of shared values, and you may be concerned about generating conflict among your allies, or ruining your reputation with them and being rejected by your group.

It's also possible that you don't really want to know what the other person has to say. You may realize you mostly want them to listen to you, and you're really not interested in listening to them. This is not a good recipe for successful dialogue. You need to truly want to understand the other person, and you need a degree of humility to believe it's as important for you to understand them as it is for them to understand you. You may have to push yourself to care about what the other person is saying and convince yourself that they have something valuable to offer.

You may feel like engaging with people across political lines is a zero-sum game in which there's no way for both people to win. If you believe that one of you must lose, you will either avoid participating in dialogue or you will try to win it, which will prevent successful dialogue. Dialogue isn't about winning. It's about understanding.

Finally, I hear people resisting the idea of being pushed into dialogue. You might fear I'm saying you have to sit through someone yelling at you, that you must allow your most deeply held values to be berated without recourse, that you cannot say what you truly believe, that you must compromise your position. To this barrier, I remind you that you get to choose whether and when you engage in dialogue and with whom. Remember, having the skills to engage in dialogue offers an opportunity, not a mandate, to do so. It's your choice.

Ideally, this book will be a resource for you as you try to address these barriers. I also encourage you to keep in mind the motivations that draw you to dialogue. Think about those motivations you identified at the beginning of the chapter: Do you want to connect, persuade, understand, collaborate, heal, reduce your distress? Remembering why you want to do this can help you persist in developing the skills to connect across political lines.

One More Barrier

In talking with people about their experiences, I have come to recognize another barrier to dialogue that typically isn't expressed outright and that is conflicting motivations within ourselves: We want more than one thing. We want to have dialogue, but we also have other wants that impede dialogue. We want to understand people who disagree with us, but we also want to say what we think. We want to see things from another perspective, but we also want validation for our own view. We want to maintain important relationships, but we also want to express our frustration. We are motivated to have dialogue, in other words, but we have other motivations as well. And these other motivations might, at times, be stronger.

What do we do if our motives are in conflict? For example, what if you're an outspoken environmentalist, and you're confronted with someone who doesn't believe in climate change? If you knew that talking about the dangers of climate change drives this person farther away from your view,[1] would you stop sharing factual information about global warming? Could you hold yourself back from posting pictures of melting glaciers? In this situation, you might find yourself in the dilemma of whether to move your views forward or to move your environmental agenda forward. What if moving your views forward moves your agenda back? What if *not* sharing your views could move the agenda forward—would you do that? What would it take for you to allow something you see as untrue to go unchallenged? What kind of payoff would it need to have? And what level of certainty would you need to have about the potential outcomes? What's your internal cost–benefit analysis?

When I started doing this work, I hadn't thought about conflicting motives as a barrier to dialogue, and I didn't realize how powerful it could be. My initial approach was to ask people at the beginning of the workshop about what motivates them to have dialogue, and then to keep coming back to it: If this is what you want, here's what you need to do. I thought it might be as simple as teaching people skills that they might not have or might not be using and encourage them to make intentional choices about what they do in dialogue. But we may not be aware of all of our motivations. Unless we're conscious of the competing wants, they may interfere with successful dialogue.

When I created "The Flowchart That Will Resolve All Political Conflict in Our Country," one of my goals was to help people be more intentional. I wanted people to make a conscious choice about whether they wanted to have dialogue across political lines and, if they did, to see that they could choose how they would engage in dialogue.

If we're not acting on intention, we may be acting on unconscious motives, distorted views of others, emotional distress, and lack of confidence in our ability to participate in dialogue. In this book, there will be opportunity to reflect on your motives, understand others, strengthen adaptive emotional responses, and develop your skills. Ideally, these will help you move toward dialogue with intention.

CELINE AND KEVIN'S MOTIVATIONS AND BARRIERS

You were introduced to Celine and Kevin in the Introduction. Reflecting on their motivations helped Kevin and Celine gain some insight into what they hoped to get out of dialogue, as well as potential barriers.

Kevin's typical mode of discussing politics is debate. He is motivated by wanting to maintain his connection with Celine but also by a desire to persuade her to come around to his side. He fears it will be difficult to agree on anything because they get their information from such different sources.

Celine has been avoiding discussing politics with Kevin as she perceives him as attacking her views. She values family and doesn't like the tension between them, so she's willing to give it a try, but she has some trepidation about Kevin pushing his ideas on her.

TWO THINGS TO DO

Keeping in mind common motivations for engaging in dialogue, what do you think might help maintain relationships, understand different views, find common ground, persuade, and reduce distress?

You might want to explain why you're right. You might want to cite research. You might want to point out logical inconsistencies. You might want to walk away. You might want to tell them that they're idiots. You can react any number of ways; however, these actions are not going to help you to reach your goals. They're not going to achieve the ends you've identified as your motivations for engaging in dialogue.

For successful dialogue across political lines, it turns out that there are only two things you need to do:

1. try to understand people on the other side and
2. help them feel safe and understood.

That's it.

Why do you need to try to understand them? I often hear from people who are mystified by people on the "other side." If desire to understand is in itself a motive for you to engage dialogue, it can be met by developing greater insight into others with differing views. Understanding people who are different from you will also help you to accomplish other goals. If you want to find common ground, you will need to understand them as well as yourself and look for commonalities. If you want to persuade, you will need to understand their beliefs and values to be effective in shifting their views. And if you simply want to reduce your distress? I find that some of the distress people are experiencing arises from being mystified about others' views and in the uncertainty about how others will act. Insight into others can alleviate some of this distress.

Why do you need to help them feel safe and understood? Quite simply, the safer and more understood people feel, the more they will be open to engaging in dialogue. When people feel confronted or attacked, they shut down and become even more committed to polarized views. When they feel safe and understood, they are less

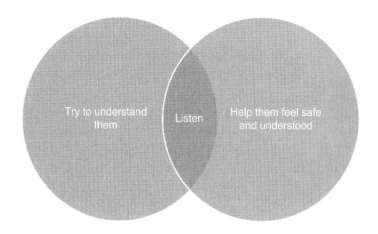

defensive, less agitated, more able to express their views, and more likely to listen to yours. They will be more willing partners in seeking common ground and less resistant to opening their minds to alternative ways of thinking.

There are a few specific skills that will help you to understand people and to help them feel safe and understood, and there's one skill that will help you to do both of those things: listening. This is the subject of the Chapter 3. But first, let's consider how to prepare for and initiate dialogue.

NOTE

1. Feinberg, M., & Willer, R. (2013). The moral roots of environmental attitudes. *Psychological Science*, *24*(1), 56–62. https://doi.org/10.1177/0956797612449177

CHAPTER 2

PREPARATION FOR DIALOGUE

How will you prepare yourself for dialogue? The answer depends on your circumstances. You may feel gung-ho to jump into political conversation with friends, family, coworkers, acquaintances, and random strangers. If so, you might decide to skip ahead to the next chapter. If, however, you're feeling some trepidation about dialogue, aren't sure how to start the conversation, or want to know how to establish the parameters of the interaction, read on.

GETTING PAST ANTICIPATORY ANXIETY

Anticipating interacting with people across political lines may feel stressful, either because you've had a negative experience or because you imagine it will not go well. It's not surprising that people sometimes avoid what they fear, but when we avoid these experiences, we do not give ourselves the opportunity to overcome our fear.[1] If you find yourself shying away from conversations with people who hold different views, it may be helpful to process distressing emotions associated with political discussions.

The feelings you experience in anticipation of dialogue may be related to past experiences of interacting with political adversaries, your personal connection to political issues, or witnessing political conflict in the media. Furthermore, whatever the actual views and intentions of the other person, your feelings about them and the feelings you think they have about you can affect your ability to engage in dialogue. You may feel like people on the other side don't value your views, don't acknowledge your contributions, don't want you to succeed. It might seem like they question your motives or your morality. Perhaps you feel attacked, invalidated, rejected, misunderstood, judged. Such vulnerable emotions can be a barrier to listening to and connecting with your dialogue partner.

Expressive writing, a type of journaling that focuses on deep feelings and thoughts, can help process distressing incidents in our past,[2] as well as reduce anxiety about future experiences.[3] Such writing, when practiced repeatedly, has been shown to have benefits, including improved physical health, enhanced relationships, and diminished psychological distress.[4] Try the activity that follows if your feelings are interfering with your ability to engage in dialogue.

Expressive Writing

1. Set aside 15 to 20 minutes of uninterrupted time in a quiet space.
2. You can write on a computer or on paper with a pen or pencil. If you're unable to write, you can record yourself speaking.
3. Write about your deepest thoughts and feelings that come up when you consider dialogue with this person, or across political lines in general. Allow yourself to let go and really explore your thoughts and feelings.
4. Don't worry about spelling, grammar, or repeating yourself.
5. Ideally, repeat this writing activity for 3 or 4 days in a row.

This activity is based on the method developed and described by James Pennebaker.[5] Additional guidance on expressive writing is available in various books, including *Opening Up by Writing It Down*.[6]

WARMING THINGS UP

Dialogue across political lines will likely be more effective, and will certainly be more pleasant, if you feel some sense of warmth, positivity, and even liking toward the other person. Here I offer some strategies that may promote positive feelings in preparation for dialogue.

When you find yourself repelled by someone's political views, you might try identifying some of their good qualities. For example, they may disagree with you on environmental regulations, but maybe they're a good parent or perhaps they do a lot of volunteer work in your community. Look for something you can appreciate about people with differing views and try to view them through the lens of positive characteristics.

You might also consider the context of their life experiences and values. You might be shocked that people could possibly think as they do, but their views may be fairly typical in their community context. Consider where they grew up and the family that raised them. What kind of work did their parents do? What ideas did they hear from their family, their friends, their faith community? Find out more about their context if that helps you soften toward them.

Some people draw on spiritual practices or teachings to keep their heart open to others. Quakers may "hold them in the light"; Buddhists might practice a *lovingkindness* meditation; Christians are advised to "love thy neighbor as thyself"; others might apply teachings related to forgiveness and nonjudgment. Is there spiritual guidance that will help you cultivate positive feelings toward a person, even amid some friction or disagreement?

Perhaps participating in activities with others will help you feel closer to them. If you have a particular person in mind, you could invite them to hike, bowl, or knit together before you approach dialogue. You could work together to plan a community event, coach little league, or put on a fundraiser. You might find creative activities, like singing or dancing, help to build a connection. Is there a common interest to work on a collaborative art project, like painting a mural or preparing a performance? If you have a broad desire for dialogue and want to get to know people with a range of political views, try volunteering or engaging in these or other non-partisan activities in your community.

INVITATION TO DIALOGUE

It takes two to tango, and the same is true for dialogue. You cannot have dialogue alone; you need a partner. Who will engage in dialogue with you?

You might already have someone in mind. Perhaps your desire to connect with a particular person motivated you to read this book. Is there a family member, friend, or coworker whose political values, views, or behaviors conflict with your own and with whom you want to have a conversation? Alternatively, you may not have a particular person in mind, but you're generally interested in having dialogue with folks who have values or experiences that differ from your own. You might find that such opportunities for dialogue arise in social situations, at work, or even with strangers, such as the person next to you on an airplane. Or perhaps you're an advocate for a specific issue, which brings you into contact with people who see things differently. Depending on these circumstances, your approach to initiating dialogue may vary.

If you want to have dialogue with a specific person, you might have had prior encounters in which discussing political issues did not go well, or you might both be avoiding these topics. If you're trying to shift an established pattern from conflict or avoidance to dialogue, you may need to reach out with an intentional and overt invitation. Here are some examples:

Invitation 1: I notice we typically don't have conversations about politics, and I would like to be able to talk about these things so it's not a barrier in our relationship. Would you be willing to have a dialogue where we both try to understand where the other is coming from?

Invitation 2: When we've tried to have conversations about politics, they haven't always gone well. I accept some responsibility for that as it's been difficult for me to keep my cool, but I've been working on managing my emotions, and I would really like to hear what you have to say. Are you open to giving it another try?

Invitation 3: It seems like we come at things from different perspectives. I realize this can cause some tension, but it might also be an opportunity to see if we can understand each other's views and maybe even find some common ground. Are you interested in seeing if we can have a conversation like that?

Of course, there are many ways of broaching the topic, and you will want to find the words that fit for you, but these examples work for several reasons. First, they frame what you hope to accomplish and how dialogue might be helpful in achieving these goals. They also comment on observable behavior rather than making assumptions about what's going on for the other person. Finally, they are not accusatory about the other person's behavior—they take a neutral stance or even accept responsibility for playing a role in prior conflict. There will be opportunity to establish communication guidelines (which are addressed later in this chapter), so it's best to find out if the other person is generally willing to participate before you put parameters on what it will look like.

You may get a variety of responses to your invitation for dialogue. Some people might be enthusiastic and eager to participate.

On the other end of the spectrum, some may be very clear that they have no interest in, or are even antagonistic about, the possibility of such dialogue. In this type of situation, it's best not to push them. You can simply say something like, "No problem, I just wanted to reach out. If you ever change your mind, let me know." Some people may have some interest but also some trepidation about dialogue. If this is the case, you can implement your listening skills by reflecting their feelings. "It sounds like you think it's a good idea, but you're nervous about actually doing it." Invite them to share more about their concerns, correct any misconceptions they have about dialogue, articulate your intentions about what you would want dialogue to be like and how you would engage, and see if that moves them toward participating in dialogue.

If the other person is willing to engage in dialogue, you can negotiate the specifics. Schedule a time when you won't feel too rushed so you can be fully present and allow the conversation time to unfold. You can also say you're open to getting together more than once if it seems like more time is desirable. It's ideal to have a face-to-face conversation, rather than one in writing—especially if the writing is in the form of comments on social media posts! If you can't arrange to be in the same room, video calls (such as FaceTime, Skype, WhatsApp, Google Hangouts, or Zoom), are options that can help you pick up on each other's non-verbal cues. In terms of location, try to select somewhere that feels comfortable to both of you, provides adequate privacy, and isn't too loud—you don't want to set up a situation where you have to shout to be heard.

You can also offer resources that will help the other person prepare to participate in the dialogue. If you find this book helpful, or if you think your dialogue partner might, you could share it. See the end of the book for additional resources that you can offer as well.

If opportunities for dialogue present themselves, less planning is required. You don't necessarily need to indicate to the other person that you're establishing a dialogue. You could simply apply the skills that will be introduced in the chapters that follow: listen, try to understand the other person, manage any emotions as they arise, and share your experiences and values. If you want to deepen or extend the dialogue, you can make a more explicit invitation.

Celine and Kevin were fortunate that their children initiated the idea of dialogue. When they saw each other at a family wedding, Kevin said, "I feel like politics have gotten in the way of our relationship, and clearly our kids want us to try talking about it. What do you think? I'm game if you are." Celine agreed, and they scheduled a time for a conversation the following week.

COMMUNICATION GUIDELINES

As noted in the prior section, Invitation to Dialogue, you may want to establish some guidelines for communication with your dialogue partner. Such parameters can help the dialogue remain civil and productive. By anticipating potential pitfalls and mutually agreeing on behaviors, both of you may feel more comfortable in the conversation. You can copy the handout of communication guidelines at the end of this book and share them with your dialogue partner in preparation for or at the start of the conversation.

If you're not sure how to bring up the subject of communication guidelines, you can always blame me! "I read this book that had some suggestions to help our conversation go smoothly" is a good lead in. If it's not feasible to set parameters before you start the conversation, you can model these guidelines and suggest them as needed during the conversation.

Respect. Demonstrating regard for people's experiences and values is vital to successful dialogue. You don't need to agree with

39

them to accept their views. You can show respect by encouraging dialogue partners to share their perspective and experiences without interruption. Also, keep in mind that when you make assumptions about people's motives, they can become defensive. It's wise to treat people as if they are intelligent, moral, and well-intentioned. When you hear something that you disagree with, you can challenge the opinion without attacking the person who holds the opinion. It's respectful to refer to people with their chosen labels: if someone considers themselves pro-life, don't refer to them as anti-choice; use the name and pronouns they indicate, even if that doesn't fit with the way you see things. Ask questions from a place of curiosity rather than judgment. Don't try to lure someone into saying something inconsistent or incorrect and then leap on them with a "gotcha." It won't help anything, and it's disrespectful.

Confidentiality. Confidentiality may help to establish trust in dialogue. If someone thinks you will represent or misrepresent to other people what they share with you, they may be guarded in terms of what they say or even in expressing emotion. It can be helpful to agree at the beginning of the dialogue on the level of confidentiality you want to maintain. Is it OK for others to know that you participated in this dialogue with this specific person? Can you share what you learned about people who hold a particular perspective without identifying the specific person? Is there anything about either of your backgrounds or experiences that you would like to be kept confidential? Alternatively, would either of you prefer for your views to be shared in an attempt to promote understanding beyond the two of you in the dialogue?

Speak from your own experience. Sometimes we fall into the habit of making generalizations about groups of people, both the ones we belong to and the ones we don't—men, women, Democrats, Republicans, people of various political views or ethnic groups. Rather than speaking about groups of people, try to speak from your own experience. This is sometimes called using "I" statements. Using "I statements" also refers to owning your feelings rather than framing your feelings as caused by someone else, such as "I feel angry when you ____," rather than, "You make me angry."

Managing discomfort. Establishing communication guidelines does not necessarily mean that everything will feel easy or that there won't be some bumps along the way. It may be helpful to keep in mind that you can each choose what to share and when. At the same time, dialogue necessitates some level of sharing, so at times you may notice discomfort, but don't allow it to stand in the way of sharing. It can be helpful to be aware of feelings and distinguish between discomfort that you can tolerate and red flags that indicate a high level of distress. Breathing or taking a break can help to regain equilibrium (see Chapter 4).

Other guidelines. Are there any other guidelines that will help to create a positive dialogue experience for either one of you?

KEVIN AND CELINE DISCUSS COMMUNICATION GUIDELINES

Here's how Kevin and Celine discussed communication guidelines.

Celine: Thanks for suggesting we talk. I've been feeling uncomfortable when we're both at family gatherings, and I have to admit, I've been sort of avoiding you.

Kevin: Yeah, I've been feeling it, too. It's been weird and tense. I know we both have strong feelings about politics, but I don't want that to get in the way of our relationship. I've always valued our connection. You were my go-to person for parenting advice when my kids were little.

Celine: True, but I don't feel like you respect my opinions anymore.

Kevin: It's been hard for me to understand where you're coming from, but I'm willing to make an effort, if you are.

Celine: OK, let's give it a try, but I don't want to get into a big argument with you.

Kevin: I don't want that either. Maybe we can have some guidelines that will help us have an easier time talking.

Celine: Like what?

Kevin: Well, even if we disagree, maybe we can try to be respectful of the other person's view. (*Respect*)

Celine: Sure, that sounds like a good idea, if you think you can manage it.

Kevin: That's definitely what I want to do, but if you feel like I'm being disrespectful, let me know.

Celine: OK, thanks. I appreciate that.

Kevin: Maybe we can also agree that if our tempers start to flare, we can call a time-out so we can simmer down. (*Managing discomfort*)

Celine: OK.

Kevin: Is there anything else that would help you to feel more comfortable?

Celine: You know, I'm a little nervous that you're going to misconstrue what I say to other people in the family. I don't want your kids to hear some crazy story about what I think.

Kevin: Yeah, I get that. I'm not sure I want everyone to hear what I say to you out of context.

Celine: So, can we agree to keep this between us? (*Confidentiality*)

Kevin: Definitely.

STRUCTURING THE DIALOGUE

In addition to the skills you've learned here, there are some ways to structure the dialogue that you may find useful. You do not have to follow this structure, and it might feel more natural for you to take a completely different approach, which is fine.

You might start out with some normal conversation—getting to know each other if you don't already, catching up if you do. An easy way to shift from small talk is to thank them for their willingness to engage in dialogue. Again, dialogue is not easy, and it can feel like taking a risk, emotionally and interpersonally. It's important to acknowledge that your dialogue partner may be stretching beyond their comfort zone to do this. If nothing else, they are taking time out of their lives to participate.

If you haven't already done so, you can discuss communication guidelines. Although you don't need to set specific goals for the dialogue, it might be nice for each of you to say what you hope to get out of the dialogue experience.

You may want to have some ideas about how to start the dialogue. "I've heard you say X. I'd be interested in hearing more about what that means to you and how you came to these views." Once things get going, your skills of listening, managing emotions, talking, and understanding others can carry you through the dialogue.

Now that you've started the conversation, where do you go from here? In the next chapter, you'll learn how to listen effectively, a key foundation for dialogue.

NOTES

1. Jeffers, S. (2007). *Feel the fear and do it anyway.* Ballantine.
2. Pennebaker, J. W., & Evans, J. F. (2014). *Expressive writing: Words that heal.* Idyll Arbor.

43

3. Park, D., Ramirez, G., & Beilock, S. L. (2014). The role of expressive writing in math anxiety. *Journal of Experimental Psychology: Applied, 20*(2), 103–111. https://doi.org/10.1037/xap0000013
4. Lepore, S. J., & Smyth, J. M. (2002). *The writing cure: How expressive writing promotes health and emotional well-being.* American Psychological Association.
5. Pennebaker, J. W. (n.d.). *Writing and health: Some practical advice.* https://liberalarts.utexas.edu/psychology/faculty/pennebak#writing-health
6. Pennebaker, J. W., & Smyth, J. M. (2016). *Opening up by writing it down: How expressive writing improves health and eases emotional pain.* Guilford Press.

CHAPTER 3

WHY LISTEN?

Most people do not listen with the intent to understand. They listen with the intent to reply.

—Steven Covey

You know those moments in conversation when you hear something you want to respond to? Suddenly you're thinking about what you want to say. You're crafting an argument, or maybe you agree with what's being said, but you want to impart some information from an article you read about it. Either way, you're focused on your own thoughts. Meanwhile the other person is still talking, but you've missed the rest of what was said. This is *listening to respond*, and it doesn't promote dialogue. In contrast, a type of listening often called *active listening* helps the listener to understand and helps the speaker to feel understood, and is a key facilitator for dialogue across political lines.

To illustrate how listening helps you understand another person, let's consider an example. Say you want to know how a television works. If you get a book that explains how televisions work, the information is available to you—but you still need to read the book. Of course, it takes some effort to read a book, but that's how you can get the information you seek. It would be pretty silly of you to sit there with the book in front of you, griping about how you can't understand how televisions work. Similarly, if you can't understand why people hold different views from yours and you have someone in front of you who holds these views, the information is available to you, but you need to access it. You might know *how to read a book*, but you might not know *how to listen* in such a way that people will share with you and that you can take in what they are saying.

None of us was born knowing how to read a book. Similarly, we weren't born knowing how to listen effectively, and it takes some effort to learn these skills. Because listening skills are helpful in a variety of contexts, you may have been exposed to them in workplace, relationship, or parenting training. There are also a variety of models of communication that emphasize listening (e.g., Marshall Rosenberg's nonviolent communication[1]). If you are already familiar with listening skills, you might simply want to consider the ways in which they can be applied to dialogue across political lines. If you haven't had training in these skills, I encourage you to take note of the guidance in this chapter and practice. Listening may not be the most exciting part of dialogue, but it is essential if you want to be successful.

You may recall from Chapter 1 that to meet your goals of dialogue, you need to understand the other person. This may be your primary goal—you don't understand why people think or act as they do, and you hope dialogue will shed some light. In this case, understanding the other person is an obvious win. However, even if understanding others is not your primary motivation, it will help you to achieve other goals. For example, you need to know where the other person is coming from to identify common interests or values. Similarly, it will be important to grasp others' point of view if you want to persuade them to change their mind.

In addition to increasing your understanding of another person, active listening can communicate to dialogue partners that you care about and understand what *they* have to say. Helping a speaker feel understood has a wealth of benefits. First, demonstrating that you understand can reduce conflict and help to build the kind of connection that promotes dialogue. If someone feels understood, they may also feel more comfortable opening up and sharing views, which in turn promotes further understanding and can help you feel greater empathy.

Think about a time you felt misunderstood by somebody. You might have felt maligned. Did you defend yourself and correct them? Or did you simply disengage? Either way, you likely didn't feel closer to and more comfortable with them. Now think of how it feels to be understood: You can relax, you want to open up, you feel more trusting. Feeling understood is healing in itself and is crucial to having the kind of connection needed to engage in difficult dialogue. By listening actively, not only do you understand the other person, but they feel understood—and feeling understood helps our defenses go down. Listening in a way that makes people feel heard will help others feel more comfortable sharing information with you, and when you are actively listening, you are more likely to take it in.

In my training as a psychologist, I spent a lot of time learning how to actively listen. You might think therapists listen to gather information, so we can offer insight or guidance. Although this is useful, it's not the main reason active listening is important. Listening helps therapists develop a supportive relationship, which is actually the greatest contributor to therapeutic healing.[2] No matter what else a therapist does, no matter what else the client does, if the therapist listens and creates a supportive environment, it helps the client heal.

This book will not teach you how to be a therapist, but it will help you to develop one of the most powerful tools that therapists use in the healing process. And this tool of active listening will help you to be effective in dialogue across political lines.

LEARNING HOW TO LISTEN

Imagine you and I are having a conversation about our children. You tell me that you're really happy with the charter school that your daughter is attending. The class sizes are smaller than her previous school, and the teachers seem really responsive to her interests and strengths. You were frustrated with the other school because it didn't seem to allow for much creativity or flexibility on the part of the students or teachers. As you talk, my eyes wander around the room, I tap my foot and look at my watch. When you're done talking, I say, "Oh. I think charter schools are a real problem." In a similar demonstration in workshops and classes, I take a vote about whether I was a good listener or a bad listener. I am unanimously elected a bad listener.

When I ask what made me a bad listener, every group picks up on my lack of eye contact, my fidgeting, my lack of response to what the speaker said. I would ask you if you felt understood. Undoubtedly, your answer would be "no."

Let's say we give it another try. This time, I face you in a relaxed but still manner, I nod, I say, "Mmmhmmm." I end by saying, "You feel like your daughter is having a good experience in her new school." We take another vote, and the outcome is overwhelmingly for "good listener." When I ask what made me a good listener, the audience identifies what I've noted here. They describe me as encouraging, warm, and open; and you would add that you felt understood. Success!

We all know what bad listening and good listening look like. Although it's more easily recognized than implemented, the research is clear that these skills can be taught.[3] Furthermore, listening is essential for dialogue that aims to foster connection, as well as that which seeks to promote learning across difference.[4] So even if it seems basic, it's important to start here because productive dialogue is not possible without listening.

NONVERBAL ATTENDING

The most basic aspect of active listening is "nonverbal attending," which is giving someone your full attention without speaking. Several skills will help you to do this effectively:

Physical stance. Keep your body open to the speaker, facing them, arms uncrossed. Try to be relaxed but attentive. If you're sitting, lean forward a bit rather than slouching back in your seat. Keep a comfortable distance—not too far, not too close. The ideal distance can vary depending on culture, gender, power, and personal preferences, so pay attention to the speaker's cues. If you keep moving closer to engage with somebody, and they keep backing up, you're probably too close. Maintain moderate levels of eye contact, looking at the speaker but not like you're competing in a staring contest.

Minimal encouragers. Simple gestures communicate to the speaker that you are listening and encourage them to continue. Head nods are one way—just don't do it continuously. No bobble-head doll imitations. Occasionally say "Mm-hmm" to communicate encouragement. The mouth-open impatience of listening-to-respond expresses, "I have something to say—can you please finish so I can say my thing?" In contrast, minimal encouragers suggest, "Please go on."

Silence. The final key to nonverbal attending is the nonverbal part. It turns out that you can't listen to somebody very well if you're talking. In fact, if you rearrange the letters of the word "listen," it spells "silent." (I can't believe it took me 20 years of teaching helping skills to discover this, but it's a useful reminder for both novice and experienced listeners.)

Offering somebody uninterrupted time to talk, even a few minutes, is a generous gift that we so seldom give each other. It doesn't mean you have to keep your mouth shut for hours and hours, but I encourage you to see how long you can simply listen to somebody without wanting to interrupt, or see how long others allow you to speak uninterrupted. This can be hard, and people are often rather stingy with listening. Seeing the impact of silent attention on a speaker—how supported they feel, how they relax—may inspire you to work on this skill and offer silent listening more often.

Some people find the most difficult part of listening is not talking. Commonly, they're worried that if they don't speak, they'll forget what they wanted to say. This leads to a choice: You get to decide if it's more important to say something because it came into your head or to build connection with the other person. You might make different choices at different times, but it's important to make conscious choices. My brain is very, very busy. If I said every single thing that went through my head, it would be a cacophony. We're always making choices about which of the things in our heads come out of our mouths. Keep in mind that every thought might not be the most important thing to express in that moment. There's a deep humility in listening because the focus is more on understanding the other person than on saying everything that comes into your mind. Remember that you want to understand and help the speaker feel understood and reserve your speech for what moves you closer to these goals.

REFLECTING

The second active listening skill is "reflecting," which is repeating or rephrasing key content or meaning from the speaker's statement. For example, if someone told you, "I just came from a PTA meeting, and I'm so frustrated with charter schools. They're draining money from the school system, which is already stretched, so we don't have the funds to support our students and teachers. Plus, they're weakening the teachers' union, and the last thing teachers need is to have less power to advocate for decent pay and benefits. I wish the charter school parents would put all that energy into supporting our existing schools instead of creating new ones that compete for resources," you might say, "So, you feel like charter schools are taking away resources from teachers and students in noncharter schools."

A reflection communicates that you heard what the speaker said, but rather than saying, "I hear you," you demonstrate that you heard them by sharing back a little of what they said. A reflection also confirms that you have an accurate understanding of the speaker. If you're a little off target, it gives the speaker an opportunity to correct you. This can be useful if you didn't quite understand what they were saying. If you say, "You think charter schools are ruining the educational system," the speaker could clarify, "Well, not exactly ruining it as much as creating challenges for the existing schools."

Reflecting typically feels more awkward for the person doing it than for the person hearing it. You may be wondering, "Won't that be weird to just repeat back what they're saying?" You might think, "They just said it—how can it be helpful for me to say it back?" What I know, and what's supported by considerable research,[5,6] is that people like having their thoughts and feelings reflected back to them.

You shouldn't try to repeat everything back. Use fewer words, and summarize rather than transcribe. I call this "nuggetizing." Get at the nugget of what they're saying. And say it briefly so you don't interrupt the flow just to demonstrate that you've heard them. Focus on something that seems meaningful to the speaker; pull out an idea that gets to the heart of what they're saying rather than focusing on a minor detail, such as "You're on the PTA."

The easiest way to reflect is simply to say it, ideally using tone or emotion that resonates with the speaker's. For example, "Teachers need to be supported." If you feel more comfortable framing it, you could preface your reflection with one of these phrases: "I hear you saying," "It sounds as though," "So . . ."

Reflecting is only one of many possible responses to a speaker's words. For example, you might find yourself wanting to go beyond what a speaker is saying. However, listening to understand does not require, or even benefit from, interpretation or moving a conversation toward a deeper level. You might think you need to say something insightful like, "So, you would advocate for policy that limits the creation of new charter schools." Whether or not this is accurate, it goes beyond what the person is saying. It is not a reflection, and it distracts from their train of thought. It's more important to simply be present than to be brilliant.

You might want to demonstrate support by agreeing: "I agree, charter schools are a bad idea." This sort of statement can be problematic because you may not agree, and even if you do agree, it puts you in an evaluative position rather than an understanding position. An evaluative position is a judgmental one, albeit frequently inadvertent. It puts the focus on your preference, and implies the importance of your judgment, rather than signaling to the speaker that you have understood their assertion. It's easy to play innocently into this habit because sharing the same opinion about charter schools sounds like you're relating positively. It's good that you're on the same page, right? The problem is that you won't always agree, and whether you agree or not, a value placed on a speaker's statement inhibits their sense of being understood for what they've said versus what you think about it.

In a different attempt, you might want to show that you're interested by asking a question: "What kind of school did you go to as a child?" This statement shows that you were listening, but it moves the conversation in the direction of your curiosity and might, in so doing, lead you to miss the chance to explore what's meaningful to the speaker.

These various alternatives to reflection may be well intentioned, but they do not fulfill the crucial role: to help people feel heard and to make sure you understand them. Reflection will help you keep it simple. Responding in more a more complicated fashion can clutter or redirect the conversation in ways that deflect from your goal.

To give you a sense for how it can work with practice, let's put it into action in another example. Consider what you might say as a reflection if someone said the following:

> I don't trust politicians. I mean, I know they can't tell us everything, but it seems like there's a lot that goes on behind closed doors. Are they really being as honest and transparent as they could be, or are they making deals that help them and do nothing for the public?

Now let's take a look at some possible reflections and evaluate them on some key criteria. When considering the following reflections, ask yourself, does the reflection do these things?

- Capture some aspect of what the speaker said
- Use fewer words than the speaker used (does it nuggetize?)
- Focus on content that seems meaningful to the speaker

Does the reflection NOT do these things?

- Evaluate what the speaker said
- Go beyond what the speaker said by interpreting or analyzing
- Ask a question

In response to the original statement, some people think to respond with questions such as, "Would you trust politicians more if they were more transparent?" This question demonstrates that you understand the speaker has concerns about transparency, but it's not a reflective statement.

Others interpret or analyze what the speaker is saying, as in, "Politicians, rather than trying to serve their country, serve themselves by trying to be reelected." This one doesn't exactly capture what they said, and it's a bit wordy.

There are also options that express agreement. For example, "Money and politics does seem to be a problem, doesn't it?" or "I don't trust them either." Although it might seem like agreeing helps to build connection, this isn't a reflection; rather, it communicates something about your own view. Before you move into seeking common ground, make sure that you reflect back what they are saying without interpreting, agreeing, disagreeing, or adding anything. Because this is how they know that you heard them.

Some people want to challenge or disagree: "You're treating politicians as a group rather than as individuals." Statements like this push back and can feel confrontational. If it's something the speaker wouldn't say themselves, it's probably not a reflection.

As you can see, there are many responses that are not effective reflections. Fortunately, there are also many good options that are. Here are some possible reflections that meet the criteria:

- "It sounds like you question politicians' motivations."
- "You think politicians aren't very trustworthy."
- "Distrust in politicians makes it hard for you to believe in them."

By now you know enough about reflecting to give it a try. I encourage you to practice in low-stakes situations so that you can acclimate to nonverbal attending and reflecting about a topic that's less challenging than politics. Whether you are using this book to help navigate a specific conversation with a particular person or are hoping dialogue will be a more substantial endeavor, you may find it useful to brush up on listening skills before you leap into politically charged topics. At the end of the book, you'll find instructions for an activity that can help you practice nonverbal attending and reflecting, or you can simply try it out in everyday conversation. Either way, take the guidance that you find works for you, and consider that practice will develop an ongoing skillset for that one conversation, and many others that follow.

OPEN-ENDED QUESTIONS

At this point, you may be feeling impatient to get to the part where you can ask questions rather than simply listening and reflecting. Questions suggest interest in what the other person has to say. Questions promise to promote deeper conversation. Questions feel satisfying. As you listen, questions pop into your head, and you want answers. It's true, questions can be very appealing, but they also have the potential to interrupt the speaker's thinking, shift the focus to the listener's agenda, interfere with connection, and derail a conversation. To use questions effectively keep a few things in mind.

First, attend and reflect before you ask a question. Understanding the speaker and helping them feel understood provides a strong foundation before you ask a question. Reflecting confirms that you grasp the speaker's meaning and offers an opportunity to correct any misperception. This is particularly helpful so that your questions can build on clear comprehension, rather than deepen misunderstanding. Furthermore, if you haven't communicated that you heard someone, they may not be inclined to open up in response to your question. You may feel like asking questions communicates your interest. This may be true, but if you attend and reflect first, a question says, "I'm interested in what you just said," rather than "I'm interested in your response to what I want to hear about."

It takes skillful listening to form a question without derailing the conversation. Although questions have the potential to communicate interest and deepen discussion, they also have the potential to bring the focus to what interests the listener more than what interests the speaker, and this does not promote dialogue. So, the first rule of questions is to attend and reflect first.

When you do ask a question to promote dialogue, it's most effective to use questions that are open-ended, that is, questions that cannot be answered simply with a yes or no. For example, rather than "Do you think public charter school should receive the same level of funding as other public schools?" which can be answered "yes" or "no," you might ask, "How do you think public charter schools should be funded?" Open-ended questions promote elaboration and exploration.

Have you ever started to ask a question without being clear on exactly what you want to ask, and the question ends up getting long and convoluted as you work it out along the way? This is not uncommon, but it's also not helpful for dialogue. It's best to keep questions brief so you don't interrupt the flow of the speaker's thinking. Lengthy or complex questions may derail a speaker who is moving toward making a point or trying to articulate a train of thought. The more airtime you occupy to ask your question, the more you draw the focus to yourself rather than trying to understand the other person. Short questions support dialogue.

Just as in reflecting, you want to keep questions simple. You may feel like you need to use complex language or deep interpretation to demonstrate your intellect or insight. In fact, these approaches may interrupt exploration and dialogue. Resist the urge to try to guide or impress the speaker with your exceptionally astute question. Simple questions are a powerful tool for exploration. One of my favorite and most concise ways to ask questions is simply to repeat back a key word with an upward intonation. For example, if somebody says, "I just feel like the world is so dangerous," you can say, "Dangerous?" By using the upward intonation, the word becomes a question. It says, "Tell me more about dangerous." Of course, you want to choose the word carefully. Try to zero in on something that has multiple meanings or that seems to carry some energy for the speaker. If somebody says, "I just feel like the world is so dangerous," and you reply "World?" it seems like you think they should be more specific than the whole world, or perhaps that you've misunderstood them to be saying that they experience Earth as dangerous, but another planet might feel really safe to them. Choosing a word that seems meaningful to the speaker will encourage them to continue on that subject.

Not all questions are really questions. On the game show *Jeopardy!*, contestants must state their answer in the form of a question. When someone says, "What is Delaware?" they don't want Alex Trebek to tell them about the first state in the Union that houses the DuPont company. The question "What is Delaware?" is really a statement. Even though the sentence ends with a question mark, it communicates an answer rather than encouraging elaboration. You may find yourself stating an answer in the form of a question when you're in dialogue. Consider questions that start with "Wouldn't you say that . . .?" or "Don't you agree that . . .?" These are not inquiries; they are statements that reflect the *asker's* view. To promote dialogue, ask questions in a neutral manner that doesn't imply agreement or disagreement on your part and that doesn't challenge the speaker's point of view. It's important to stay neutral in both tone and content. Judgment and opinion come across loud and clear in tone. Saying, "Is *that* where you're going on vacation?" is more contentious than "Tell me how you chose to go there for vacation" (which is a statement that is really a question).

In sum, to be effective for dialogue, questions should be open-ended, short and simple, and neutral. Think you've got it? Then get ready for a pop quiz!

Pop Quiz

Which of these is the best open-ended question?

A. Were you angry about the outcome of the 2016 election?

B. What were you feeling after the 2016 election? Were you upset, and was that because you were upset about what Trump would do, or was it because you felt attacked because you voted for Trump, or was it concern about the deep divide among people in our country? I mean, there were lots of different reactions—what was yours?

C. How did you react to the outcome of the 2016 election?

D. Don't you think we should get rid of the Electoral College?

If you picked C, you chose well. C is open-ended: It's short and simple, and it doesn't take a position or make any assumptions. A isn't open-ended, as it can be answered with a yes or no. A is also not neutral, as it focuses on one emotion: anger. But since people may have felt a lot of things—fear, relief, confusion, affirmation—the question may not lead them to express these feelings. B is neither short nor simple. Although it ends in an open-ended question, the path it takes to get there can derail the conversation and make it difficult to respond. D is not a neutral question, and it is not open-ended. It is a statement of opinion with a question mark at the end, don't you think?

Open-ended, short, simple, and neutral are guidance about *what* you ask. It's also important to think about *when* to ask it. The first rule of timing: Don't interrupt just to ask a question. Do you ever find yourself listening to someone, and a really great question pops into your head? But they keep talking without a pause, and now they're onto the next topic, and you haven't asked your amazing question yet? It might even be difficult to focus on what the person is saying because you're thinking about your question, and you're afraid that if you don't ask it, you'll forget it. So you go ahead and ask it. Now doesn't that feel better? Well, yes and no. It might feel better for you, but it probably doesn't feel better for the other person because what you've communicated is that you think your question is more important than what they saying, which might discourage them from talking with you. Best to keep the focus on what they're saying and let your question go. It might turn out that there's an opportune moment to ask it later, or it might even be that forgetting your wonderful question isn't so terrible after all. There are cultural variations related to the regions we come from to consider in the ways we speak to each other. For instance, when my New Yorker friend interrupts his North Carolinian wife to ask questions or to agree with what she is saying, she finds it very annoying and sometimes has to ask him to stop. However, when he is with other New Yorkers, it feels to him as if it's the norm to interrupt each other, and in fact, he sometimes gets nervous and wonders what others are thinking when the conversation is devoid of interruption. Although we may be used to speaking and listening from habit and cultural influence, when considering the conscious conversation that political dialogue invites, the skill-building here is grounding to the process and necessary. You can hone these skills with an activity at the end of the book that brings together nonverbal attending, reflection, and open-ended questions.

CELINE AND KEVIN APPLY LISTENING SKILLS

What happens in a typical conversation about politics that doesn't use nonverbal attending, reflecting, and open-ended questions? Let's listen in on a conversation Celine and Kevin had last year about health care, before they read this book:

> *Celine:* I just renewed my health insurance, and I can't believe how much it costs! Wasn't Obamacare supposed to be affordable? It was obviously a huge failure.

Kevin: But it does make it affordable for millions of Americans who couldn't get health insurance otherwise! I thought you didn't even have health insurance before. Isn't it better to know you're covered in case something happens?

Celine: No, I'd rather keep my money and use it to stay healthy and pay my own medical bills. Why should I have to pay for insurance if I don't need it? I take care of myself—I don't smoke, I work out, I eat healthy. It doesn't seem fair that I do all that, and I'm paying a ton so I can support a guy who drank himself into a liver transplant.

Kevin: It's not like everyone who needs health care is at fault. Are you saying my mom was to blame for her heart attack? That's harsh. And there's no way she could have paid the hospital bill herself—it was huge, and the insurance company wouldn't cover the whole thing—we're still disputing it. And my mom is so worried about the money. It can't be good for her health.

Celine: See, health insurance doesn't work. We need to let people make their own choices.

Kevin: That's not what I'm saying. We need to regulate how much hospitals can charge. We need a single-payer system.

Celine: Oh, great, socialized medicine. More government interference—just what we need.

Kevin: So, what's wrong with socialized medicine?

Celine: Our taxes would double, and the quality of health care would plummet.

Kevin: That's ridiculous. Where are you getting your facts?

As you can see, the conflict between Celine and Kevin is escalating. With each interaction, they challenge each other, and their tone becomes more abrasive. They might be getting their ideas out there, but it's likely going to take a toll on their friendship: Celine may complain to mutual friends that Kevin is a socialist, and when Kevin's mother's health declines, he might not reach out to Celine.

Imagine Kevin had used nonverbal attending and reflection to listen to Celine:

> *Celine:* I just renewed my health insurance, and I can't believe how much it costs! Wasn't Obamacare supposed to be affordable? It was obviously a huge failure.
>
> *Kevin:* Mm-hmm
>
> *Celine:* I mean, forcing everyone to get insurance, and then we have these crappy choices that cost a fortune. This is exactly why we shouldn't have government interfering where it doesn't belong.
>
> *Kevin:* You're pretty upset about how much you're paying for health insurance.
>
> *Celine:* You bet I am! I mean, why should I have to pay for insurance if I don't need it? I take care of myself—I don't smoke, I work out, I eat healthy. It doesn't seem fair that I do all that, and I'm paying a ton so I can support a guy who drank himself into a liver transplant.
>
> *Kevin:* You do a lot to stay healthy, and you resent that other people don't.
>
> *Celine:* Exactly.

In this exchange, Celine expressed the same views as in the previous example, but Kevin used active listening. Kevin's minimal encourager (mm-hmm) and reflections (*You're pretty upset about how much you're paying for health insurance* and *You do a lot to stay healthy, and you resent that other people don't*) allowed Celine the space to talk without being challenged. It might be hard for Kevin to keep his views to himself, but he'll have a chance to talk in a moment. He's starting off the conversation by building the relationship and helping Celine feel understood. Now, let's see how it works to combine all of these listening skills: nonverbal attending, reflecting, and open-ended questions. Back to Celine and Kevin's conversation—this time, Celine is listening:

> *Kevin:* I agree that Obamacare isn't great. I think private insurance companies are a lousy way to provide health care coverage. They spend all this money on marketing and paying shareholders, which jacks up the cost of medical care, and then they don't even pay when you need them.
>
> *Celine:* Mm-hmm
>
> *Kevin:* When my mom had a heart attack last year, the hospital bill was outrageous. The insurance company wouldn't cover the whole thing, and we were left with this huge bill—we're still disputing it. And my mom is so worried about the money, it can't be good for her health.
>
> *Celine:* Sounds like it's been pretty stressful.
>
> *Kevin:* Definitely. It's been such a mess.
>
> *Celine:* I get that you feel like the current insurance system isn't working. How do you think health care should be covered?
>
> *Kevin:* I really like the idea of the government overseeing the health care system, a single-payer plan.

That way, they could regulate the medical costs
and cut out the insurance company profits that
should have no place in health care.

Celine: So you think we should all be covered under a
government-run health insurance plan.

Kevin: Exactly.

In this exchange, Celine used a minimal encourager (mm-hmm)
and reflections (*I get that you feel like the current insurance
system isn't working* and *So you think we should all be covered
under a government-run health insurance plan*) to demonstrate
that she understood Kevin. Plus, her reflection, *Sounds like it's
been pretty stressful*, communicated empathy about Kevin's
mother's illness and financial troubles. Even though they disagree,
by expressing caring, this exchange could help Celine and Kevin
maintain, and even deepen, their connection. Both the reflections
and Celine's open-ended question (*How do you think health care
should be covered?*) encouraged Kevin to elaborate on his views,
which can be helpful to promoting mutual understanding.

OVERCOMING COMMON BLOCKS TO EFFECTIVE LISTENING

With this example of Celine and Kevin, you can see how minimal
encouragers, reflections, and open-ended questions can help people
talk about politics while maintaining positive relationships.
Although these might seem like simple skills, it's not always easy
to shift conversational habits to actually use active listening. Most
of us have never received training in communication and are ill-
prepared for how challenging it can be to implement these skills.
Here is some guidance on addressing some of the most common
stumbling blocks to effective listening.

Reflecting feels unnatural and awkward.
Don't feel bad if you can't do it right away. It's not uncommon for reflecting to feel unnatural if you're not used to doing it. The good news is that it gets easier. Remember when you first learned how to drive a car? At first, you were conscious of your every action: keeping your hands on the steering wheel, checking the rearview mirror, signaling, keeping the appropriate distance between you and the car in front of you. You had to think about each element as you were doing it. But now, driving has become fairly automatic. Not only can you drive without thinking, you can focus on other things while you're doing it—listening to music, asking your phone for directions, talking to your kids in the backseat. Learning to listen is a lot like this. At first, you may have to concentrate hard to pick up on key content, and paraphrasing it may not feel smooth. This awkwardness may deter some people from reflecting. My best advice is to just keep doing it. With practice, you will get better, it will be easier, until eventually it feels like normal conversation.

To practice your listening skills, start easy. Practice in solid, trusting friendships and relationships, with people you're relaxed around and who will forgive you for mistakes. Don't practice it for the first time in the midst of a conflict with someone. And although your goal in learning these skills is to generate dialogue across political lines, those aren't necessarily the best *practice* situations. Practice in low-stakes conversations about noncontroversial topics with people who help you feel at ease. Set yourself up for success.

Reflecting is one of the most helpful things you can do to build a connection with someone. If you don't believe me, try an experiment. In everyday conversations with your friends, coworkers, partner, or children, occasionally reflect back what they say. I expect you will find that they respond positively. It's a little bit magical how much people appreciate being heard and understood.

What should I do if someone won't stop talking?

The great thing about effective listening is that it encourages people to talk. But people sometimes worry that they will encourage people to talk and talk and talk. In some circumstances, this is great. The speaker is taking advantage of the opportunity to deepen their and your understanding, share their experiences, and fully articulate their views. But what do you do when someone is just rambling, not saying anything very meaningful or jumping from topic to topic?

When a speaker is going on and on, first you need to discern whether it's a problem. If the speaker is sharing productively, give them space to continue. If you've allowed them time to express themselves, but they keep talking and don't seem to be getting anywhere, you might want to intervene. In this circumstance, you might try inserting a reflection of something that seemed meaningful. I sometimes find this easier if I preface it with "Let me make sure I understand what you're saying," or "Can I interrupt you for a minute to make sure I got this?" Sometimes people keep talking because they're not sure if you understood, so reflecting can confirm that you do.

What if someone has gone on for a while and said so much that it's hard to capture in a brief reflection? Perhaps they're telling you how concerned they are about the economy, and they've been talking for 20 minutes, telling you eight different stories about people they know who have lost their jobs. You may worry because you can't remember all the details—their friends' names and where they worked and such. Keep in mind, you don't need to summarize everything. Focus on something meaningful or related to the original topic. You might say, "You feel like the economy's in bad shape because so many people you know are losing their jobs." If they've done a lot of topic jumping, you might help them get back on track by saying, "Earlier you said . . .," and bringing them back to their original thoughts.

What should I do if the speaker doesn't talk?

On the other end of the spectrum are people who don't say much, even when you reflect and ask open-ended questions. How do you listen to taciturn speakers?

First, get comfortable with silence. You may realize that you're used to conversations where there's very little empty space and in which speakers interrupt or overlap each other. Offer the speaker some space before you talk. You may find that they have more to say or that the slower pace of conversation allows them time to think and to speak more deeply. In one of my workshops, a participant realized their enthusiasm was interfering with their listening. They felt curious and wanted to ask a lot of questions, but they realized they needed to give the other person enough space to speak. They learned to take a breath and pause before swooping in with questions. If silence is difficult for you, pay attention to your breath, and see how many you can take before the silence becomes intolerable for you. This may help you keep an accurate sense of how much time has actually passed.

Second, it may help to recognize that people are different in terms of how verbal they are. Culture, personality, and relationship between speakers shape how we express ourselves. Angela Antenore, a professional consultant and friend of mine, describes two types of communicators: "Some people think in order to speak, and some people speak in order to think." People who think in order to speak may mull things over before sharing a well-formulated idea but may never articulate all of what they're thinking. People who speak in order to think process their thoughts out loud, so they may share emerging but incomplete ideas and possibly even contradict themselves along the way to their final conclusion. The former may require more time before speaking, whereas the latter may benefit from more time for uninterrupted speech. You may be able to get a sense of which type of person you're listening to and adjust your approach accordingly.

I ran into a woman who had attended my workshop, and she told me she tried using these listening skills while talking with her daughter. She said her daughter recognized that she was using active listening and "called her on it." It's true, not everyone loves being actively listened to. In some circumstances, trying to draw someone out may feel intrusive or pushy to them. People also may not respond positively to active listening if they want to state their views briefly and aren't interested in considering or expressing their ideas in more depth. Opening up a space for listening is only useful if someone wants to move into that space. Silence and reflection invite elaboration and exploration, which is not a process everyone wants to engage in, and in such cases, active listening may create discomfort. If you're not sure why someone isn't responding well to your active listening, you might say something like "I'm curious if you would like to say more about your thoughts on this." In response to such a question, people may respond with their thoughts, or they may say something about how they're feeling about sharing their thoughts. Either way, you will have a better understanding of what's going on with them. And wasn't that your goal, after all?

When do I get to talk about my views?

You may find yourself getting impatient with listening. You want to know if you have to listen endlessly or if you get a turn. There may be a point at which the conversation seems unbalanced, where it feels like you're just a sounding board for the other person and not achieving the goal of sharing back and forth. Here are a few recommendations for when you find yourself in this situation.

First, learn to recognize how much time has actually passed. Some people who try out these skills tell me their greatest insight is how hard it is for them to stay quiet and simply listen. If you're one of those people, not talking for 3 minutes may feel like an eternity. You might try practicing in noncontroversial conversations, timing yourself to see how long you can listen without talking, and striving to extend the length of your listening span.

Second, keep in mind that your goal is to deepen your understanding of the other person. If you're not at the point where you've developed a full, rich sense of your dialogue partner's perspective, try listening more before you move to sharing your perspective.

If you've been listening and reflecting for a while (say, 10–15 minutes), and you have a clear sense of where the speaker is coming from, you may start to feel like they are monopolizing the conversation. In this case, you might want to openly discuss the process. As you do so, it's important to maintain an open tone rather than to voice frustration. Perhaps say something like, "I feel like I've gotten a better understanding of where you're coming from on this issue. Would this be a good point to shift, and I can share a bit about my views?"

If you're concerned about imbalance of airtime, you might also intentionally structure a conversation, so each person has equal time. It's best to take a moment to discuss this and agree before you start the conversation, then set a timer for a specific amount of time, perhaps 5 minutes, and take turns speaking and listening for that length of time. You may find yourself able to listen more easily, knowing that you'll have your opportunity to speak.

What if I can't think of a question?

If you have a hard time coming up with a good open-ended question, remember that you don't even have to ask questions! If you believe the best thing you can do to understand someone is to ask questions, you may jump into questions too quickly and ask too many of them. Truly, though, all you need to do is listen and reflect. So if it's hard to think of an open-ended question, just don't ask one.

You might rely on questions less as you increase your focus on listening and reflecting. One woman shared with me her observation that the speaker she was listening to answered her questions before she could ask them. The questions in her head are a sign of her inquisitive mind, but she realized she didn't need to guide the conversation—her curiosity was satisfied by simply allowing the speaker space to share. Another person noticed that when they paused to come up with a good question, the speaker continued speaking, and the listener realized that, though the pause wasn't that long, it felt long. This is a good reminder to allow silence to give ourselves and the speaker space to think.

What if, despite what I've said about not needing to ask questions, you really want to ask a question but it's difficult to come up with one? You can always try a reflection such as, "You said your parents taught you to care about the environment," and follow it up with "I would be interested in hearing more about that." Although it's not technically a question, a statement of your interest has a similar effect of encouraging someone to say more about a particular thing.

CELINE AND KEVIN PRACTICE LISTENING

As Kevin and Celine begin their dialogue, they apply listening skills from this book.

> *Celine:* So, what should we talk about?
>
> *Kevin:* I've been feeling pretty fired up about immigration, and I'm having a hard time understanding people who are on the other side of this issue, so maybe we can start there.
>
> *Celine:* Sure, why don't you start by telling me where you're coming from? (*Open-ended question*)
>
> *Kevin:* Well, I keep seeing these pictures in the news of children in cages, and it's so distressing. I mean,

can you even imagine someone separating you from your kids and putting them in cages? I would completely lose my mind! (*Celine uses silence and nonverbal attending.*)

Celine: It's really upsetting for you to think about your own kids in that kind of setting. (*Reflection. Although Kevin has posed a question, it seems like he's expressing his opinion rather than seeking input, so Celine continues to reflect rather than respond.*)

Kevin: Of course it is, but it's not just that. These people are fleeing horrible conditions in their own countries, and U.S. policy has destabilized some of these countries, which has made them less safe for the people who live there. Don't we have an obligation to help them? (*Celine uses silence and nonverbal attending.*)

Celine: If we've contributed to the problem, we should help solve it. (*Reflection. Celine simply states Kevin's perspective, although if she felt uncomfortable saying it in a way that it may appear that she agrees with this sentiment, she could preface it with "You feel like . . ."*)

Kevin: Exactly. Also, this is a country of immigrants. Most U.S. citizens are descendants of people who came to this country to flee persecution or for a better life. Who are we to slam the door behind us? (*Celine uses silence and nonverbal attending.*)

Celine: It sounds like you see limits on immigration as hypocritical. (*Reflection*)

Kevin: Yeah, that's right, I do. Thanks for listening to my views. I want to hear your thoughts, too.

(Kevin feels heard and provides an opportunity for Celine to share.)

Celine: Well, I agree that it's hard to see kids suffering, but I don't think we should reward their parents for bringing them into this situation. Our immigration system is broken, and until we fix it, we can't just allow everybody in. Our system can't handle it. I know our family came to this country once upon a time, but things have changed since then. Back then, people settled the land and built the infrastructure of this country. Now, people are being resettled in established communities and drawing on the resources of the people who already live there. I want to make sure we have enough resources for the people who have invested in our system before we start giving it away to outsiders. *(Kevin uses silence and nonverbal attending.)*

Kevin: So you feel like immigrants are taking away resources from our communities, and there's not enough to go around. *(Reflection)*

Celine: Right. It's unbelievable how many students are in a classroom. And teachers have to deal with so many issues with kids who don't speak English and who move from school to school that they don't have as much attention for the other students. *(Kevin uses silence and nonverbal attending.)*

Kevin: You know, even though we have really different views on this, it seems like we both care about children and want to make sure they're treated well. *(Reflection)*

> *Celine:* Yes, I'm glad you see that. I'm so tired of liberals accusing conservatives of not being compassionate.
>
> *Kevin:* It's really helpful for me to hear more about where you're coming from. It makes it easier for me to understand how you're coming from a caring place.
>
> *Celine:* Thanks. Thank you for hearing me out. It's a wonderful surprise to feel heard and acknowledged by someone with a different view as strong as yours.

As you can see, Kevin and Celine each came to a deeper comprehension of the other's views, even though they continue to disagree. Furthermore, they both appreciated feeling understood.

FINAL THOUGHTS ON LISTENING

When you truly listen, you might hear things you don't want to hear. If you give others uninterrupted time to speak, they may say things you find incorrect or hurtful or offensive. If you reflect their perspective rather than sharing your own, you may feel like your views are unheard. If you ask a genuinely open-ended question, the speaker may go in a different direction than where you might have wanted the dialogue to go. All of this may make you feel powerless or vulnerable.

In a courtroom drama, lawyers use questions to lead the witness to a foregone conclusion. The vulnerability of listening comes from letting go of control of the conversation by allowing the speaker to lead the way. Planning exactly what you want to say and saying it helps maintain control, and this may feel like the safest option, especially when you're feeling vulnerable. It is not, however, dialogue. I once said to my therapist, "I don't mind being vulnerable as long as I know the other person will respond with kindness and support." She wisely replied, "That's not being vulnerable." And it's true, vulnerability is not knowing how the other person will respond but making space for it anyway. We need to embrace, or at least tolerate, this vulnerability if we want to understand another person more than we want to advocate for our own perspective.

The final thing to keep in mind about attending, reflecting, and open-ended questions is that these tools are employed to help develop connections to promote understanding. The connection is the important thing; you don't need to prove you're using each of these tools to get there. So if the tools aren't working in a certain situation or if you have the connection without the tools, don't force yourself to use them. That said, don't underestimate them either. These tools are backed by research and experience, and they can help you navigate the unpredictable, challenging waters of dialogue across political lines.

In this chapter, you learned the importance of listening to help a speaker feel understood and tools to establish connection by listening. It may have felt like exercising a lot of patience and sitting with unheard feelings in response to a speaker's assertions. You may wonder how Kevin and Celine remained so calm when faced with opposing views. The next chapter, "Managing Emotions," will help you engage with feelings that come up in dialogue, manage conflict, and keep the dialogue moving in a productive direction.

NOTES

1. Rosenberg, M. (2015). *Nonviolent communication* (3rd ed.). Puddle-Dancer Press.
2. Lambert, M. J., & Barley, D. E. (2001). Research summary on the therapeutic relationship and psychotherapy outcome. *Psychotherapy*, *38*(4), 357–361. https://doi.org/10.1037/0033-3204.38.4.357

3. Darsten, M., Lisper, H., & Sohlberg, S. (1979). Learning of active listening and a comparison between students in psychology and experienced psychologists' empathetic understanding. *Scandinavian Journal of Behaviour Therapy, 8*(1), 13–21. https://doi.org/10.1080/16506077909456123
4. Wahl, R. (2019). Just talk? Learning across political divides on college campuses. *Theory and Research in Education, 17*, 139–164. https://doi.org/10.1177/1477878519862546
5. Kornhaber, R., Walsh, K., Duff, J., & Walker, K. (2016). Enhancing adult therapeutic interpersonal relationships in the acute health care setting: an integrative review. *Journal of Multidisciplinary Healthcare, 9*, 537–546. https://doi.org/10.2147/JMDH.S116957
6. Weger, H., Jr., Bell, G. C., Minei, E. M., & Robinson, M. C. (2014). The relative effectiveness of active listening in initial interactions. *International Journal of Listening, 28*(1), 13–31. https://doi.org/10.1080/10904018.2013.813234

CHAPTER 4

MANAGING EMOTIONS

Let's try an experiment.

Imagine a conversation across political lines that goes badly. What's your worst fear of what *un*civil discourse would be like? Maybe the other person is agitatedly expressing their views with voice raised, face flushed, and looking like a bull about to charge. Perhaps someone is misunderstanding you, questioning your motives, hurling explosive accusations: "How could you believe that?!" "Children are suffering, and you don't care!" "People like you are ruining our country!" Take a moment to conjure this scenario up in your mind—try to picture this person, hear their voice, feel the heat of their breath as they rage at you. You might want to close your eyes to envision them vividly. Try to experience this encounter as viscerally as you can.

Now, notice what's going on inside you. Bring your awareness to your body—your heart rate, your breathing, your muscles. Pay attention to your emotions: What are you feeling? What kind of thoughts are going through your mind?

Next, I want you to blow some bubbles. Imagine I've handed you a bottle of bubbles, and pretend you're blowing through a little plastic circle covered in soapy film.

As you blow imaginary bubbles, again observe your internal experience. What's going on in your body, your emotions, your thoughts? How do they compare to a moment ago, before the bubbles?

When people try this experiment, they often describe initial physical feelings of increased heart rate, muscle tension, shallow breath, clammy or sweaty palms, flushed. They express fear, anxiety, frustration, and feeling unsafe. They may have thoughts of yelling back, striking out, or of escape: "I need to get out of here." Some feel so overwhelmed that they dissociate, or feel disconnected from their bodies and their thoughts. Did you describe your experience in similar ways?

After blowing bubbles, people report that they feel their breathing deepen, their muscles relax, their minds clear. They have regained a sense of calm, of equilibrium. You may notice these changes, as well. Bringing awareness to your breath may make you conscious that you hadn't been breathing before. You might notice that you feel lighter, more spacious, open. Perhaps there's a smile on your face. Do these responses resonate for you?

FIGHT, FLIGHT, FREEZE

These reactions to a threat are not at all surprising if you keep survival of the fittest in mind. Humans are designed to survive dangers that were present in the environment thousands of years ago—think saber-toothed tigers. Imagine you're living during the Old Stone Age, about 30,000 years ago. Wearing a fur-lined tunic made of animal skin, you spend most of your days gathering plants and firewood, crafting stone tools, hunting big game, and, in your down time, painting the inside of the cave where you sleep. You're out hunting and gathering one day when a saber-toothed tiger leaps out of the bushes. What do you do?

76

Maybe you hoist your spear, growl, and run toward the tiger. This is the "fight" response. Another option is to turn around and run as fast as you can. This is flight. The physiology of fight and flight are similar. In either case, your heart rate increases to pump blood to your extremities, and your breathing becomes more rapid to provide oxygen to your muscles[1] so you can act, to help your legs run faster, your arms attack with greater strength. This is the sympathetic nervous system at work. It's what kicks into gear when you're in distress, when you need sympathy.

The sympathetic nervous system might give you the ability to outrun or overpower the tiger. Or it may not. Some animals respond to fight by attacking back, and they may chase fleeing prey. A third option is to lay down and "play dead" or freeze. Freezing in response to threat can work in situations where trying to escape or doing battle would be ineffective.[2] Sometimes immobility is adaptive; the tiger might eat you, but it might simply leave you alone.

These responses helped our ancestors survive. Those who did not have the instincts to fight, flee, or freeze were eaten by the tiger, and their DNA died with them.

What does this have to do with dialogue across political lines? You will not encounter a saber-toothed tiger these days, but our

FIGHT   FLIGHT   FREEZE

bodies continue to perceive and respond to threat based on this old wiring. And someone with whom you're experiencing conflict is perceived by your body as a threat. In fact, your reactions to simply imagining such conflict in the experiment at the beginning of this chapter likely elicited fight, flight, and freeze responses—heart racing, shallow breath, fear, frustration, desire to escape or shout back.

The perceived threat may be due to the forceful quality of their speech. You may be reading nonverbals. You may feel threatened because the content of their views challenges your choices, identities, or lifestyle. You may also feel threatened because you imagine them to be potentially explosive or violent based on the people in the media who express similar views.

If you respond to dialogue across political lines based on fight, flight, or freeze, this is what it might be like:

Fight is when you attack back. This could look like yelling at the other person, venting your frustration, and speaking your views forcefully. But there is a difference between venting and dialogue. You need to choose which you want to engage in. Sometimes you may want to argue with someone who disagrees with you, which is fine, but know that you're not engaging in dialogue, and you will likely not achieve your goals.

Flight is when you get the heck out of there. You can take flight, and there may be situations where this truly is the best option—where you don't feel like dialogue is productive, you know you'll blow your top, or you're emotionally depleted. Then you might choose to seek solace among people who are on your same wavelength, to get comfort and nourishment. And perhaps try dialogue again some other time or with some other person.

Freeze is where you feel so overwhelmed that you can't do anything. It's the equivalent of lying down and playing possum. When you're too overwhelmed to act, you just shut down. Either way, you aren't in a position to engage in dialogue.

It might seem disproportionate to equate a saber-toothed tiger with a conversation partner speaking their views forcefully. However, when your body perceives a threat, it instinctually responds with fight, flight, or freeze. Fortunately, although humans are guided by instinct, we are not at the mercy of it. Your body may not distinguish between lethal threat and verbal conflict, but your mind can. If you are aware of and can anticipate how your body responds to stress, you're in a better position to make a choice about how to respond.

FORWARD

Rebound Versus Reaction

There may be times when fight, flight, or freeze are the best options, but what if they're not the path you want to take? How do rebound rather than react? There are ways to shift what's going on in your body and your mind that will counteract these reactions. I call this path *Forward*.

Let's consider what happens in the body after you've escaped the saber-toothed tiger. Your body cannot sustain its current state— heart racing, shallow breath, flushed; it would be impossible to focus on a task, to sit calmly, to think clearly. Indeed, this state puts a great deal of pressure on your body, and it would be damaging to continue to experience this level of stress.

When we move from a threatening to a neutral or relaxed circumstance, our parasympathetic nervous system helps our body return to a calmer state. When the brain no longer perceives a threat, hormone levels adjust, which brings down the heart rate, slows breathing, relaxes muscles, and lowers blood pressure.

We can support the parasympathetic nervous system's efforts to move our bodies out of fight, flight, or freeze. By calming ourselves when we're in situations that feel threatening but are not actually physically dangerous, we strengthen our capacity to face challenging situations and bounce back from hardship. Such resilience will be helpful in dialogue across political lines, as well as other life challenges.

Awareness

The first step is awareness. Simply noticing our physical sensations, emotions, and thoughts can assist us in moving out of fight–flight–freeze. Consider the people I asked to imagine a conflictual conversation. They reported what was going on in their bodies, their feelings, and their thoughts. Before I asked, though, they hadn't noticed—they were too caught up in the experience of the conflict. You might have had a similar experience—your muscles tight, your breathing shallow, but you didn't notice until I brought your attention to it.

It's great if you were able to notice your thoughts and feelings when prompted. This helps you get to know what stress feels like for you, which will help you to recognize it when it's happening, and even anticipate it. The next step is to prompt yourself, to be aware of what's going on internally without someone else asking. The more readily you're able to do this, the better. If you can notice that your body is responding to stress, you're in a better position to take action to shift your internal state, which can help you to interact more effectively in dialogue.

Grounding

When the sympathetic nervous system kicks into gear, you can harness your body's ability to curb the fight–flight–freeze reaction. One of the most effective ways to do this is through a process called *grounding*, to establish calm and focus. Breathing is one of the easiest ways to ground.

When you breathe slowly (6–10 breaths per minute is optimal), you stimulate the parasympathetic nervous system, which returns your body to a state of equilibrium.[3] Try putting your hands on your stomach, then feel your belly extend when you inhale, and move back toward your body as you breathe out. Now you're practicing *diaphragmatic* breathing. This deep breathing method is particularly helpful.

You might think of this slow, deep breathing as "bubble breathing" because it's how our breath works when we blow bubbles. The great news is that we breathe all the time, so you can use this tool without it being obvious to the person you're in dialogue with. Ideally, you'll practice when you're not in dialogue so you can use bubble breath effectively when you need it.

When you're actually in dialogue, all you need to do is (a) remember to breathe and (b) breathe. The more you practice, the easier it will be to do both. Although actually blowing bubbles in someone's face may, of course, escalate conflict, you may find it helpful to imagine you're blowing bubbles, both to deepen your breathing and to help lighten the intensity of the experience. Breathing deeply, slowly, and rhythmically will calm you. It will help you to feel safer and more able to engage with the other person.

Grounding can also be achieved by focusing on physical sensations. If you're feeling overwhelmed by emotions, paying attention to the body can help you shift into the present moment.[4] Simply noticing your body's contact with the floor or a chair can help your body stay out of fight–flight–freeze. You can also bring attention to the feeling of your hands resting in your lap or folded around each other, and then you can put some gentle pressure on your legs

Practice Bubble Breathing

Before you try this, get some bubbles for a fuller experience of this exercise.

1. At first, simply bring your attention to your breath. Don't try to change your breathing, just be aware of it. Notice the pace of your breath: Are you breathing quickly, slowly, or somewhere in between? How deep is your breath? Are you breathing into your lungs or all the way down into your abdomen?

2. Now, try blowing some bubbles. If you don't have any handy, you can imagine blowing bubbles. As you blow, notice the pace and depth of your breath. Are there any changes? Many people notice that when they blow bubbles, their breath is slow and deep.

3. Next, practice without the bubbles. Count to 5 as you inhale, and then count to 5 as you exhale. This will keep your breath slow and steady. Notice the feeling of your breath through your nose or across your lips. Try to deepen your breath into your abdomen. You can place your hands on your belly to feel the air pushing your stomach out as you inhale, and releasing your stomach inward as you exhale.

4. Finally, picture yourself in heated conversation with someone across political lines. Imagine what they're saying, the tone and volume of their speech, and how they look. Now notice your breathing and any tension in your body. Either with or without bubbles, try to slow and deepen your breath while continuing to imagine this heated conversation. See if you can keep this image in your mind while breathing slowly and into your abdomen.

5. Practicing bubble breathing when you notice tension in your body will help prepare you to calm yourself during dialogue across political lines or in any stressful situation.

or give your hands a little squeeze to ground yourself. Grounding techniques can be useful for people who are experiencing posttraumatic stress, as well as other overpowering emotional states, and you may find it useful if dialogue starts to feel too intense. It's helpful to practice these techniques on your own so that you're prepared to implement them when faced with political conflict. Mindfulness meditation can be an effective way to strengthen your ability to ground yourself in such stressful situations.

Shifting Our Minds

There are also ways to shift out of fight–flight–freeze by changing our mental view of the situation—shifting our perceptions and interpretations.

For example, you could recognize that you're faced only by a human being, not a tiger. And that even if you feel like your life is in danger, likely the worst thing that will happen is that someone will disagree with you and maybe speak to you in a harsh tone . . . loudly. That's not a pleasant experience, but it's not a physically threatening one in most situations (see *Noting the Emergency Exits* later in the chapter for what to do if you think you are actually in danger).

You can also find a phrase that helps you maintain your sense of calm and focus. You might repeat in your head that the person in front of you is "not a tiger, not a tiger." You can remind yourself that you're safe by thinking, "I'm okay. I'm okay. I'm okay." Take a moment now to find a word or short phrase that feels calming and comforting for you.

It may also be helpful to remind yourself why you chose to be in this dialogue. Drawing on your motivation can help you believe that it's worthwhile to remain engaged, even if it's challenging. For example, people sometimes say they want to be in dialogue because they have a hard time understanding how people can think, vote, or believe as they do. If this is true for you, and you have someone in front of you who can help you understand, it may be helpful to remind yourself that you really do want to hear what they have to say so you can understand them better.

Flexibility

Some people, especially those who are engaged in advocacy, push back against this idea of remaining calm. They feel like they're constantly embattled, and they're tired of being reasonable. They hear people speaking in opposition to their views, their values, and even who they are as people, and they don't want to be nice. They're frustrated, and they feel justified in blowing their top.

In these situations, I think about the lesson we teach children about using their "inside voice." Playing outside, it may be fine for them to be loud and boisterous. But when they come inside, adults may encourage them to use their "inside voice," to speak more quietly and calmly. Distinguishing between inside voice and outside voice helps children develop awareness of different contexts and the type of communication that's appropriate in each circumstance. The better they are at matching their voice to the context, the more effective communicator they will be.

The most effective advocates modify their communication depending on the audience. When speaking with others in your cause, rousing speech that conveys your views emphatically may solidify commitment and inspire action. However, this same style of communication may be off-putting to those who do not share your perspective. Recognizing these different contexts and modifying speech accordingly can promote effective dialogue that will support your goals. Moreover, being outraged takes a toll on your body, especially if you maintain anger or frustration for prolonged periods of time. So it's not only a matter of how the other person will react to you; it's also important to take care of yourself by managing your emotions.

Flexibility is helpful—not only in outward behavior but also in expectations. When approaching dialogue with a very specific vision for an acceptable outcome, we may be frustrated when things don't turn out exactly as we had hoped. Let's say you're seeking common ground with a friend on gun control, and after lengthy conversation, the only thing you two can agree on is that guns exist, but you are completely at odds about whether and how they should be regulated. In these circumstances, you may feel like the dialogue has failed and that you've put in a lot of effort for nothing, which can be frustrating.

We know from psychological research that the more flexibility we have in the outcomes we desire, the lower our distress.[5] In the same vein, the Dalai Lama is said to offer this pithy wisdom: "Attachment to outcome, big problem." In other words, if you get attached to a particular outcome of a conversation, you're much more likely to get frustrated if it doesn't go precisely in that direction. At the same time, you have motivations that bring you to dialogue—to heal a relationship, to persuade, to cultivate understanding—and you may feel like if you can't achieve these goals, why bother engaging in dialogue?

What I like to think about is that there's a sweet spot where you can hold your motivation for engaging in dialogue across political lines without getting attached to a specific outcome of that conversation. Perhaps you can be open to a range of options, including simply remaining calm when talking with a person whose views push your buttons. Dialogue across political lines can be challenging, and it's important to set reasonable goals that we can achieve, even if these goals are not your ultimate vision for what you hope to accomplish. Such flexibility in desired outcomes will help you reduce your distress and remain engaged in dialogue.

KEVIN AND CELINE MANAGE EMOTIONS

In Chapter 3, Celine and Kevin used listening skills. They seemed to do a remarkable job keeping their cool, even when they were hearing potentially provocative statements from each other. How did they manage to remain calm? Let's revisit their dialogue, but this time, we'll take a look at what was going on internally for each of them:

> *Celine:* So, what should we talk about?
>
> *Kevin:* I've been feeling pretty fired up about immigration, and I'm having a hard time understanding people who are on the other side of this issue, so maybe we can start there.
>
> *Celine:* Sure, why don't you start by telling me where you're coming from? (*Celine feels a little nervous to share her views because she's not sure how they'll be received. She notices her heart beating a little faster.*)
>
> *Kevin:* Well, I keep seeing these pictures in the news of children in cages, and it's so distressing. I mean, can you even imagine someone separating you from your kids and putting them in cages? I would completely lose my mind! (*Celine thinks, "Of course you would lose your mind! That's why you wouldn't endanger your children by bringing them on a dangerous journey to another country that's not prepared to house them! What are these parents thinking?" She feels the urge to counter Kevin's statement with her own views. Then she remembers how important family is to her. She keeps her thoughts to herself and tries to focus on hearing what Kevin has to say.*)

Celine: It's really upsetting for you to think about your own kids in that kind of setting.

Kevin: Of course it is, but it's not just that. These people are fleeing horrible conditions in their own countries, and U.S. policy has destabilized some of these countries, which has made them less safe for the people who live there. Don't we have an obligation to help them? (*As Kevin becomes agitated, Celine can feel her face getting flush, and she wants to run. She recognizes that her sympathetic nervous system is activated. She brings her awareness to the feeling of the chair beneath her to ground herself, and she takes a slow, deep breath as she continues to listen.*)

Celine: If we've contributed to the problem, we should help solve it.

Kevin: Exactly. Also, this is a country of immigrants. Most U.S. citizens are descendants of people who came to this country to flee persecution or for a better life. Who are we to slam the door behind us? (*Kevin's positive response to her reflection helps Celine relax a little. She continues to focus on her breathing.*)

Celine: It sounds like you see limits on immigration as hypocritical.

Kevin: Yeah, that's right, I do. Thanks for listening to my views. I want to hear your thoughts, too. (*Kevin is feeling encouraged by the dialogue so far and is ready to listen.*)

Celine: Well, I agree that it's hard to see kids suffering, but I don't think we should reward their parents for bringing them into this situation. Our immigration system is broken, and until we fix it, we can't just allow everybody in. Our system can't handle it. I know our family came to this country once upon a time, but things have changed since then. Back then, people settled the land and built the infrastructure of this country. Now, people are being resettled in established communities and drawing on the resources of the people who already live there. I want to make sure we have enough resources for the people who have invested in our system before we start giving it away to outsiders. (*As Celine starts speaking, Kevin feels attacked, and he can hear the blood pulsing in his ears. He notices his impulse to interrupt her and argue but realizes he's having a "fight" response. He reminds himself that he truly wants to know what she thinks and that he's not in physical danger. He calms himself by repeating her childhood nickname in his head, "Cece, Cece, Cece."*)

Kevin: So you feel like immigrants are taking away resources from our communities, and there's not enough to go around.

Celine: It's unbelievable how many students are in a classroom. And teachers have to deal with so many issues with kids who don't speak English and who move from school to school that they don't have as much attention for the other students. (*Kevin wants to blurt out, "Those poor kids! Of course they need attention after all they've been through! With all the resources*

*our country has, how can you deny them that?"
but he manages to hold back. It dawns on
Kevin that he probably won't be able to persuade Celine—they're coming from such different views. He reminds himself to be flexible
about the outcome of this dialogue and notices
some common ground.)*

Kevin: You know, even though we have really different
views on this, it seems like we both care about
children and want to make sure they're treated
well.

Celine: I'm glad you see that! I'm so tired of liberals
accusing conservatives of not being compassionate. (*Kevin thinks, "Well, you don't sound very
compassionate right now," but he knows that
saying this will halt the connection they're developing. He stops himself, takes a breath, and finds
some appreciation for the conversation they're
having.*)

Kevin: It's really helpful for me to hear more about
where you're coming from. It makes it easier
for me to understand how you're coming from a
caring place.

Celine: Thanks. Thank you for hearing me out. It's a
wonderful surprise to feel heard and acknowledged by someone with a different view as strong
as yours.

Kevin and Celine have been through a roller coaster of emotions inside, but they have managed to remain calm and present in
their interactions with each other. As you can see, this is not so easy.
It requires consistent awareness of and attention to the thoughts and

feelings that arise. If you're not experienced with these strategies, practicing them in less charged situations can be helpful preparation for dialogue across political lines.

DEESCALATING CONFLICT

Now that you know how to manage your emotions, you may be wondering what to do if the person you're talking with doesn't manage theirs. Here you are breathing and thinking, "not a tiger, not a tiger," and remaining flexible, and you're faced with someone who is flushed, speaking forcefully, and clearly upset that you don't agree with them. Is there anything you can do to help them move out of fight–flight–freeze?

The good news is that the best thing you can do to deescalate conflict is to listen and respond empathically,[6] and you already know how to do this! That's right, use the skills you learned in Chapter 3 to help the speaker feel like you care and understand. Your supportive, genuine, nonjudgmental response can reduce aggressive behaviors. It's also important that your message, tone, and nonverbal actions are calm and nonthreatening, which is great because you can apply the skills in this chapter to help the other person feel safe. If these strategies don't work, you may want to end the conversation, and you can find guidance for doing so in the section that follows.

People sometimes ask me if they should use humor to lighten the mood. Although it's a good idea to try to shift the energy, others may experience humor as disregard for the seriousness of their experiences or values, so I typically caution against it. Use humor only if you have a trusting and respectful enough relationship with the other person that humor won't damage the connection you're building.

NOTING THE EMERGENCY EXITS

What if you barely begin to dialogue and you notice yourself feeling unsafe? Or if you find yourself in a conversation you aren't ready for? We'll take a moment here to interpose an escape hatch.

A participant in one of my workshops recounted a distressing situation in which she was driving her supervisor to a work-related activity, and the supervisor was vehemently spewing his political opinions, which she did not agree with. Because she was in a moving car, she did not feel like she could leave, and because it was her supervisor, she did not feel like she could disagree with him or ask him to stop. She felt trapped and vulnerable. This is the kind of situation that would benefit from an escape hatch. I suggested she could say something like, "I appreciate that you shared with me some of your thinking. I think what will help me focus on my driving right now is to put on the radio." So even if you're stuck in the same physical space with somebody, you may still be able to get out of this conversation without going into the reasons why.

Of course, the situation just described is not dialogue as defined in Chapter 1. It sounds more like diatribe. The problem here is not about dialogue across political lines; it's a problem of a supervisor inappropriately inflicting their views on a subordinate in a workplace situation. When there is unequal power, the person with less power may feel threatened, especially if they feel trapped, demeaned, or belittled for their views. If you find yourself in such a situation, do not hesitate to end the conversation, if you're able to do so. If you do not feel like you can end the conversation, use the skills in this chapter to manage your distress until you're able to remove yourself from the presence of the other person. If you feel like you're in physical danger, don't worry about being polite—just get yourself out as quickly and safely as you can.

Keep in mind that you have a choice about whether, how, and when to engage in dialogue. As I said at the beginning of this book, knowing how to have dialogue offers an opportunity, not a mandate, to do so. In any given situation, you get to weigh your motivations against the challenging internal and external reactions that you may experience in dialogue, and you get to decide what you want to do. You get to decide if you want to conclude, "I'm noticing my reactions and I actually don't want to participate in this dialogue." Or you might decide, "I'm noticing my reactions, and I want to work with those reactions and see if I can calm myself and keep trying to do this." And I'm not saying one of those is right or wrong because it depends very much on the situation—how threatening it feels, what your relationship is like with that person, and how much progress toward your goals you feel is possible. There are a lot of reasons you might choose one or the other, but recognize that you get to make a choice.

In Chapter 8, you'll find the activity "Scripting Your Exit" to help you find your own words for bringing dialogue to an end, to effectively close out situations that feel unsafe, or to exit exchanges you don't want to engage in.

INDIVIDUAL DIFFERENCES IN MANAGING EMOTIONS

It's important to acknowledge that everyone has a different threshold for rebounding. These variations are dependent on a number of factors, including environmental sensitivity (biological wiring), experiences of conflict and trauma, dynamics of the relationship in which the dialogue is occurring, lifetime experiences of power and vulnerability, investment in and personal experiences with the topic being discussed, practices we've developed to manage our emotions, and situational factors (such as what else has happened that day).

People who have experienced trauma may have a particularly difficult time remaining calm in the face of perceived threat. As adverse childhood experiences, or ACEs, are becoming more widely acknowledged and understood, the physiological and psychological impact of trauma is more apparent. Children whose homes feel like a constant interaction with a saber-toothed tiger have difficulty soothing themselves, and this difficulty can extend well into adulthood. Awareness, grounding, and shifting the mind are still recommended therapeutic approaches; however, additional guidance and practice may be needed in some circumstances. Books that may be helpful are Nadine Burke Harris's *The Deepest Well: Healing the Long-Term Effects of Childhood Adversity*[7] and Linda Graham's *Bouncing Back: Rewiring Your Brain for Maximum Resilience and Well-Being.*[8] Self-compassion is also important for people with a trauma history. If you're trying and having difficulty succeeding in managing your emotions during dialogue, it's important not to beat yourself up over it. Keep in mind that your past has not set you up to succeed, and it's wonderful that you're making the effort to shift deeply embedded emotional patterns.

EMOTION REGULATION

You can think about the skills you've learned in this chapter as adaptive emotion regulation strategies, which modify your emotional state. Awareness can help us to accept our feelings. Flexibility and exiting with intention are ways of problem-solving. Shifting our minds changes our view of the situation, which is also known as reappraisal (see Chapter 5 for information that may promote reappraisal).

In contrast, maladaptive strategies, such as suppressing, avoiding, and ruminating, are associated with emotion dysregulation. Consistent use of maladaptive strategies can contribute to mental health problems, such as depression and anxiety. However, if we alleviate stress by accepting our feelings, changing our view of the situation, and problem-solving, these adaptive approaches to coping may promote good health, relationships, and academic and work performance.[9]

Application of emotion regulation strategies to dialogue across political lines can help you have a more positive experience of dialogue. You can also apply them in other stressful situations to strengthen resilience and well-being.

Emotion regulation necessitates a certain type of focus on the self. Self-awareness and self-soothing enable you to identify and rebound from physiological response to stress and support the listening skills you learned in Chapter 3. As you saw with Celine and Kevin, this can help you minimize reactivity as you are exposed to opposing views. How might increased awareness of your dialogue partner further support successful dialogue? The next chapter will help you recognize perceptions, cultivate openness, and learn about others' (and your own) moral foundations in relation to dialogue.

NOTES

1. Gordan, R., Gwathmey, J. K., & Xie, L. H. (2015). Autonomic and endocrine control of cardiovascular function. *World Journal of Cardiology, 7*(4), 204–214. https://doi.org/10.4330/wjc.v7.i4.204

2. Schmidt, N. B., Richey, J. A., Zvolensky, M. J., & Maner, J. K. (2008). Exploring human freeze responses to a threat stressor. *Journal of Behavior Therapy and Experimental Psychiatry, 39*, 292–304. https://doi.org/10.1016/j.jbtep.2007.08.002

3. Russo, M. A., Santarelli, D. M., & O'Rourke, D. (2017). The physiological effects of slow breathing in the healthy human. *Breathe, 13*, 298–309. https://doi.org/10.1183/20734735.009817

4. Center for Substance Abuse Treatment. (2014). Screening and assessment. In *Trauma-informed care in behavioral health services* (Treatment Improvement Protocol Series, No. 57). Substance Abuse and

Mental Health Services Administration. https://store.samhsa.gov/ product/TIP-57-Trauma-Informed-Care-in-Behavioral-Health-Services/SMA14-4816

5.   Bonanno, G. A., Papa, A., Lalande, K., Westphal, M., & Coifman, K. (2004). The importance of being flexible: The ability to both enhance and suppress emotional expression predicts long-term adjustment. *Psychological Science, 15*, 482–487. https://doi.org/10.1111/j.0956-7976.2004.00705.x

6.   Price, O., & Baker, J. (2012). Key components of de-escalation techniques: A thematic synthesis. *International Journal of Mental Health Nursing, 21*, 310–319. https://doi.org/10.1111/j.1447-0349.2011.00793.x

7.   Burke Harris, N. (2018). *The deepest well: Healing the long-term effects of childhood adversity.* Houghton Mifflin Harcourt.

8.   Graham, L. (2013). *Bouncing back: Rewiring your brain for maximum resilience and well-being.* New World Library.

9.   Aldao, A., Nolen-Hoeksema, S., & Schweizer, S. (2010). Emotion-regulation strategies across psychopathology: A meta-analytic review. *Clinical Psychology Review, 30*, 217–237. https://doi.org/10.1016/j.cpr.2009.11.004

CHAPTER 5

CULTIVATING UNDERSTANDING

Who are you talking with when you imagine dialoguing across political lines? Is it someone you know well, like your brother-in-law or an old friend? Or an acquaintance, someone you met at a party or the parent of your child's friend? A politician or celebrity you've never met? Or is it an entire category of people, such as Democrats, Republicans, environmentalists, Evangelical Christians, pro-choice advocates, NRA members?

Take a moment to reflect on them. What do they look like? Where did they grow up? What do they do with their time? What are their positions on policy issues? What values do they hold and why?

If you want to have dialogue with people across the political divide, it is helpful to have a clear idea of who these people are. Although we cannot really know them unless we connect with them as individuals, there are ways that we can prepare ourselves to understand them fully. This chapter offers several tools to cultivate empathic and accurate perceptions of those who have views and values that are different from our own.

DISTORTED PERCEPTIONS

A study conducted in the 1990s examined the views of pro-choice and pro-life college students as well as their perceptions of each other.[1] Participants read written descriptions of women who were seeking abortions; some of these women were depicted in more sympathetic situations, and some less so. Researchers then asked them to indicate how sympathetic they felt toward each woman. They also asked them to rate how sympathetic they thought a typical pro-choice and a typical pro-life person would be. See Figure 5.1.

Not surprisingly, the pro-choice people were overall more sympathetic to the scenarios (A) compared with the pro-life people (D). What's interesting is that pro-choice people were overall *less* sympathetic than pro-choice people *assumed* pro-choice people would be (B), and they were also less sympathetic than pro-life people assumed pro-choice people would be (C). So, both pro-choice

FIGURE 5.1. Actual Versus Expected Sympathy Ratings

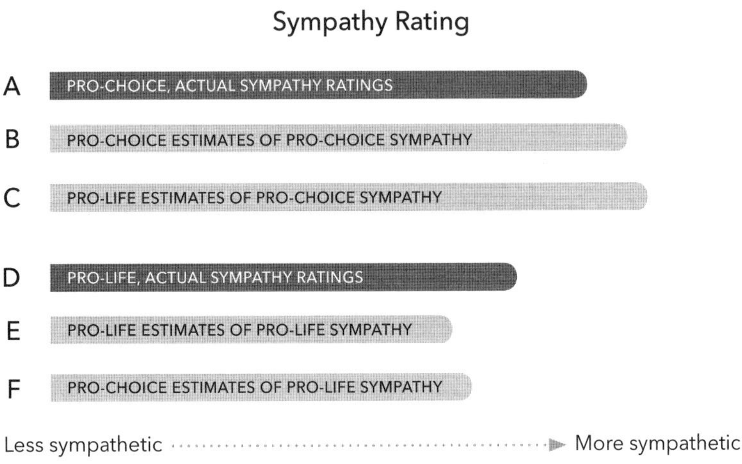

Sympathy Rating

A PRO-CHOICE, ACTUAL SYMPATHY RATINGS

B PRO-CHOICE ESTIMATES OF PRO-CHOICE SYMPATHY

C PRO-LIFE ESTIMATES OF PRO-CHOICE SYMPATHY

D PRO-LIFE, ACTUAL SYMPATHY RATINGS

E PRO-LIFE ESTIMATES OF PRO-LIFE SYMPATHY

F PRO-CHOICE ESTIMATES OF PRO-LIFE SYMPATHY

Less sympathetic ···▶ More sympathetic

Note. Data from Robinson et al. (1995).

and pro-life people thought pro-choice people were more extreme than pro-choice people actually were. Similarly, pro-life people were *more* sympathetic (D) than pro-life (E) or pro-choice (F) people thought pro-life people were.

What that means is that the actual divide between pro-choice and pro-life people is smaller than it's believed to be. People on each side tend to overestimate these three disparities: the gap between the two sides, the gap between their own personal views and what they think the views of the other side are, and the gap between the people who are on what they perceive to be their side and people who they perceive to be on the other side of things.

Perhaps you're not convinced by this one study from decades ago that was done with a small sample of college students about a single issue. If you need more proof that we overestimate the political divide, you might be interested in the American National Election Study, a survey regarding various political issues that is conducted every other year across the United States. An analysis of more than 20,000 responses to this survey from 1968 until 2008 reveals a striking pattern regarding the perceived and actual political divide.[2] It turns out there has been a real increase in political polarization over 3 decades; however, people perceive polarization to be greater than it is across time and across issues, including health care, aid to minorities, and defense spending. The researchers found that polarization is particularly exaggerated if you identify strongly as either a Democrat or Republican and if you consider those whose views you're estimating to the "opposing group."

In Figure 5.2, the bars represent the actual range of views people hold, the dots on the left are the positions people think Democrats hold, and the dots on the right are the positions people think Republicans hold. As you can see, the actual distance between views is less than the perceived distance on all of these issues across 30 years of research. So, this tendency to overestimate the distance

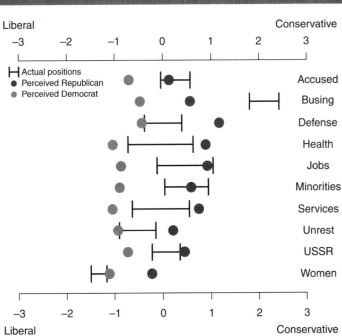

FIGURE 5.2. American Perceptions of Polarization

Note. From "Perceiving Political Polarization in the United States: Party Identity Strength and Attitude Extremity Exacerbate the Perceived Partisan Divide," by J. Westfall, L. Van Boven, J. R. Chambers, and C. M. Judd, 2015, *Perspectives on Psychological Science, 10*(2), p. 148 (https://doi.org/10.1177%2F1745691615569849). Copyright 2015 by Sage. Adapted with permission.

between our own views and those of people on the other side is consistent and persistent.

One reason we overestimate the political divide is that extreme views are more commonly represented in the media, including social media. One study[3] looked into political views of the general U.S. public via surveys with a representative sample of 8,000 people.

They found that people clustered into seven categories based on core beliefs, sense of group belonging, and political behaviors. Descriptions of the categories are also based on in-depth interviews with people in each category. Although there are people at both extremes, most of the respondents fell into what they described as the *Exhausted Majority*. See Figure 5.3. These folks in the middle are disinterested and disengaged in politics due—in part, to the conflictual tone of people on the extremes. We are less likely to hear from them than from those on the extremes.

Our distorted perceptions are not only about the distance across the political divide, we also view the motivations of those on the other side differently than we view our own. Remember the

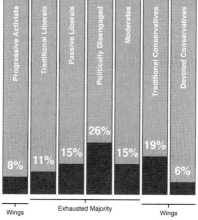

Note. From *Hidden Tribes: A Study of America's Polarized Landscape* (p. 6), by S. Hawkins, D. Yudkin, M. Juan-Torres, and T. Dixon, 2018, More in Common (https://hiddentribes.us/pdf/hidden_tribes_report.pdf). Copyright 2018 by More in Common. Adapted with permission.

study about pro-choice and pro-life college students? The authors of the study pointed out that people believed that their own views were influenced by objective or pragmatic concerns, whereas they thought those who disagreed with them were more shaped by political ideology. They even thought that other people on their own side were more shaped by political ideology than they, themselves, were. So, basically everyone thinks that they are making very rational decisions about things but that nobody else is, even people who agree with them. *Naïve realism* is this tendency of human beings to think that our views are well supported and that other people's views are not. Furthermore, people's tendency to believe that people on their side are motivated by love, and people on the other side are motivated by hate appears to be at the root of some of the world's most intractable conflicts.[4]

APPLYING A CORRECTIVE LENS

Chapter 2 contained suggestions for generating warmth, but you may have found it challenging to implement these ideas due to your assumptions about people who hold political views that differ from your own. The research presented earlier in this chapter may encourage you to question these assumptions. Simply realizing that your views about others may be distorted can help you feel more openness toward them.

We typically find it easier to give someone the benefit of the doubt if we think they will do the same. However, in times of political polarization, it's hard to believe people on the "other side" could think well of us. Keep in mind, though, that we tend to distort views of people across political lines. Their animosity toward us, as well as our animosity toward them, may be rooted in these distorted understandings of each other. Thus, moving out of conflict may require opening ourselves to clearer perception of them and allowing ourselves to be seen by them. And they may feel more open toward us when we demonstrate warmth—when we show that we are not the enemy and that we don't think they are either.

PERSPECTIVE TAKING

It is obvious that we spend most of our lives seeing things from our own perspective—understanding our own views within the context of our own values and experiences. In conversation with others, we typically share our own perspective—we say what we think and why we think we're right.

In contrast, perspective taking is about seeing things from somebody else's view: not evaluating what they're saying through our own lens, but truly attempting to understand them as they

Note. Artwork by Lisa Slavid, creator of *Peadoodles*™.

understand themselves. Perspective taking requires both the skill to understand others accurately as well as the motivation to do so.[5] Whatever your motivation for dialogue—whether you want to find common ground, persuade, stay connected to someone, or gain insight into those who disagree with you—it's useful to be able to see things from the other person's perspective.

There are many ways to put yourself in someone else's shoes.[6] Some strategies are particularly useful when you can interact with the person (or type of people) whose perspective you want to understand. First, it's important to really focus on the other person with no distractions. Second, staying calm and keeping an open mind about what the other person is thinking or feeling can also be helpful. Encourage the other person to share their thoughts and feelings by asking questions or sharing your own. You may find it helpful to communicate in multiple or rich ways. For example, brief written messages through social media or text message provide only limited information, whereas you can gain information about tone from a phone conversation and facial expressions through face-to-face conversation. You might notice that you can apply what you learned in Chapters 3 and 4 to help with perspective taking when you are in dialogue with someone.

There are some additional strategies you might useful for perspective taking if the person you want to understand is not available to interact with you, or in preparation for interaction. If this is the case, you can try to infer what someone may be thinking or feeling by reflecting on something in your own life that's similar to their experience. You might also look for differences between your own circumstances and theirs. You can ask yourself what it might be like to be someone with their experiences and values in various situations. The following exercise may be helpful in perspective taking regarding political issues; there's a version at the end of the book you can try with a partner.[7]

Practice Perspective Taking

1. First, choose an issue to focus on. You'll have an opportunity to express your views about something you feel strongly about (e.g., abortion, climate change, immigration). It may be particularly helpful to choose something for which you have strong feelings about people who are on the "other side" of the issue. Take a moment to think of what you want to focus on before you move on.
2. Now write for 3 to 5 minutes about people who believe in the opposing position. Allow yourself to express as much anger, frustration, or confusion as you feel.
3. Next, pretend you are the person on the other side. Try to imagine what they think and feel about people like you. Write for 3 to 5 minutes as if you were them writing about people who hold your beliefs. Express yourself with as much anger, frustration, and confusion as they might feel about you.
4. Now, you're back to being yourself. Write as many reasons as you can think of that someone might hold views on this issue that are different from your own. You might consider their experiences, values, or other things that would lead them to different conclusions on this issue.
5. Consider how you felt about people on the other side of this issue before you did the activity, and reflect on how you feel about them now. Do you notice any new insights about them or any shift in your feelings toward them?

LEARNING ABOUT OTHER PEOPLE

Sometimes other people's circumstances seem so different from our own that it's hard to imagine their perspective. Furthermore, you may not have easy access to these people or you may not feel confident that you can have a productive dialogue if you aren't familiar with their upbringing, beliefs, or experiences. In these situations, it can be helpful to learn about people through memoir or models.

Memoir can offer rich insights into other human beings. Personal storytelling reveals not only the external circumstances but also the inner experience of people's lives. Although one individual's story does not necessarily generalize to everyone else with a similar upbringing or experience, it can give us a glimpse into a world that's different from our own. You might seek out a memoir of someone whose experiences you are struggling to understand. The popularity of *Hillbilly Elegy*[8] following the 2016 election may have been driven by people on the political left trying to understand voters in rural America. Perhaps you can't imagine what it's like to be transgender or a police officer or a refugee. Maybe you don't know anyone who is an Evangelical Christian or who has had an abortion. I personally love to listen to audiobooks of memoirs where the author is also the narrator so I can truly hear their voice. Other books offer insight into groups of people based on research. Arlie Hochschild's *Strangers in Their Own Land: Anger and Mourning on the American Right*[9] is one example that speaks to current conflicts in the United States.

In addition to stories about people's lives, there are conceptual models that paint a picture of types of people. For example, unless you're a sociopath, whether you're on the political left or right, you have morals. People on different ends of the political spectrum prioritize moral values in different ways, however.[10] If you're on the political left, you likely prioritize sympathy, compassion, nurturance, rights, and justice; if you're on the political right, you're more likely to prioritize loyalty, obligations, authority, traditions, social order, and purity. Although both liberals and conservatives vary with respect to moral foundations,[11] a general understanding of differing priorities may offer new insights into the "other side."

You may find yourself reacting negatively to aspects of morality that are not your priorities. If you feel it is important for people

Moral Foundations	
Left/Liberal	**Right/Conservative**
Sympathy	Loyalty
Compassion	Obligations
Nurturance	Authority/Respect
Rights	Traditions
Justice	Social Order
	Purity/Sanctity

to be self-sufficient, you might feel like government policies over-emphasize nurturance, although you might also connect with nurturance if you think about it in terms of members of a community helping each other. People on the political left often cringe at the idea of "purity," but then I ask them to consider how much they value organic, non-GMO foods. It can be helpful to try to relate to the moral foundations that are not those we prioritize.

Understanding people in the context of their own morality, rather than our own, can help us to be more respectful of others' motivations, and respect is a key ingredient of successful dialogue. Furthermore, if you are interested in trying to persuade others who disagree with you, you are sure to be more successful if you frame your arguments in terms of their moral priorities rather than your own.[12]

The study described earlier in this chapter, in which the *Exhausted Majority* was identified, elaborates on characteristics of people across the political spectrum. The report based on this study (which is freely available online at http://www.MoreInCommon. com) offers insight and descriptions into people who represent each category: Progressive Activists, Traditional Liberals, Passive Liberals, Politically Disengaged, Moderates, Traditional Conservatives, and Devoted Conservatives. Reading it can help you to understand not only those whose views differ dramatically from your own but also those whose voices are typically silent on political issues.

Stereotypes are overgeneralized beliefs about categories of people,[13] and they can interfere with productive dialogue. To the extent that you hold stereotypes of people whose political views are different from your own, you may assume your positions are too far apart to even approach them for dialogue, you may harbor negative feelings toward them, you might make assumptions about them that keep you from developing an accurate understanding. As novelist and essayist Chimamanda Ngozi Adichie says, "The problem with stereotypes is not that they are untrue, but that they are incomplete. They make one story become the only story."[14] Even as you gain an understanding of various types of people who hold certain views, keep in mind that each person has their own experience, and dialogue can help you move beyond stereotypes to a full and accurate understanding of a person.

HOW TO BE RIGHTEOUS WITHOUT BEING SELF-RIGHTEOUS

Righteousness is often evoked within the context of religion to mean morally correct or right with God.[15] To be righteous is to act in ways that would be justifiable to a higher power or ethic. It is based in deeply held values and a desire to act in accordance with a virtuous path.

In contrast, people who are self-righteous view themselves as morally superior to others.[16] This feeling of superiority may be based in one's own evaluation of being more intelligent, more aligned with God, more caring, or more virtuous compared with others. Self-righteousness tends to be viewed in a negative light and may be associated with hypocrisy and intolerance for other's views. It is possible to behave in righteous ways but to also be self-righteous due to feelings of superiority for one's righteousness. How is it possible to achieve righteousness without being self-righteous? The ideal might be virtuousness without elevating oneself over others for it. As you learned in this chapter, human beings tend to attribute their own behavior to rational and loving motives while evaluating others as driven by irrational and hateful tendencies. These unconscious psychological biases offer a foundation for self-righteousness. Thus, we need to make efforts to combat these tendencies, and humility can help us to do that.

People with a high degree of cultural humility are open to hearing others' beliefs and are likely to prioritize connections with other people over proving the superiority of their own views. Even people who have strongly held beliefs can demonstrate cultural humility.[17] One aspect of cultural humility is intellectual humility, "the ability to regulate one's need to be right, respond nondefensively when one's perspective is challenged, and express curiosity, interest, and a willingness to learn about alternate points of view."[18] Intellectual humility is the recognition that one's beliefs or opinions may be fallible and acknowledgment of one's own limitations in evaluating evidence. This type of humility accounts for psychological biases that are beyond our awareness and is particularly salient to dialogue across political lines.[19] People who demonstrate intellectual humility, who recognize that their beliefs might be wrong, can tolerate ambiguity and are more attuned to the strength of persuasive arguments than those who are low on this characteristic.[20]

How can intellectual humility benefit dialogue across political lines? Dialogue involves listening and perspective taking. Some people have expressed to me that they fear if they listen without contradicting, they might legitimize the other person's perspective. Furthermore, there's some risk in listening to and understanding others that we might glimpse an idea that makes sense to us, we might resonate with something on the other side, we might change our minds. Intellectual humility can create space for uncertainty and shifting views. It can enable us to be brave and flexible, to move forth into dialogue knowing that challenges to our views won't break us. Equipped with intellectual humility, we can hold multiple possibilities, respecting all perspectives, valuing all experiences. It gives us space to learn and grow together. Perhaps you think intellectual humility sounds nice but it isn't your natural tendency. Maybe you feel defensive when your views are challenged and feel argumentative rather than curious when faced with opposing views. Although intellectual humility may come more easily to some people than others, studies show it can also be cultivated. In one study, intellectual humility increased when people were exposed to the concept of a growth mindset, the idea that your intelligence can be developed (in contrast to the assumption that intelligence is a fixed characteristic).[21] People who view intelligence as something that can be fostered have less of an investment in defending their views and more of an interest in growing their understanding. So, reading about support for a growth mindset (for example, Carol Dweck's *Mindset*[22]) can support intellectual humility. Another study demonstrated that even unconscious exposure to concepts related to humility reduced aggressive behavior toward people who had opposing views and were critical of the participant's beliefs.[23] In fact, simply reading this chapter could strengthen your capacity for intellectual humility, which may help you to be less defensive and more open to hearing views different from your own.

CELINE AND KEVIN DEMONSTRATE CULTURAL HUMILITY

In the previous chapters, Kevin and Celine used listening skills and emotion regulation to discuss immigration. How might cultural humility influence where they go from here? A few weeks after their initial dialogue session, Celine invites Kevin to a coffee date.

Celine: Kevin, I really appreciated our conversation on immigration. It helped me to feel more connected to you again.

Kevin: Thanks, Celine. I feel the same way. It was helpful to understand where you're coming from.

Celine: Your openness to dialogue gave me the idea to reach out and ask your thoughts on a topic my friends and I have been discussing. I'm curious to hear a different perspective.

Kevin: Sure, I'm happy to talk. What's going on?

Celine: Well, you know how there's so much talk about gender these days? A friend of mine, her kid is going through something. Her daughter—beautiful girl—cut off her hair and started dressing like a boy, and now she wants everyone to call her "they." My friend called a group of us moms together for support. We all seem to be on the same page about this, but I thought it might be helpful to hear a different view.

Kevin: Sure, I can share my perspective, but do you want to tell me where you and your friends are coming from first? I'm interested to hear.

Celine: It's just already so confusing for teens. They're going through so much trying to get through school and figure out their futures, and the friend drama, and the who-likes-who drama. And it's not like when we grew up—there's alcohol and drugs everywhere, and they have to walk through metal detectors just to get to class, and everyone has ADHD or anxiety. I just keep thinking, do they really need to mess with their gender in the middle of all this? You know what I mean?

Kevin: Yeah, I get that adolescence is a confusing time, and I know how much you care about kids. The way I think about it is that maybe it's less confusing if you're not trying to fit yourself into a box that's not the right one for you. But I'm curious to know what you're hearing from your friends.

Celine: I appreciate what you're saying about round holes and square pegs. That's not all there is to it, though. It's like there's pressure on everyone to experiment with gender. Kristy—that's the daughter—started hanging around with some new friends who are all into this, but honestly, she had never said anything about it before; there was no indication that being boyish is her true self. My concern is that they're too young to commit to something so big, change pronouns, let their schools know to treat them like this now. It's harder for kids to shift back if they change their mind. I have heard that from several parents. But what do you make of all this?

Kevin: I think sometimes kids don't show us their full selves if they don't think we'll accept them. Maybe they're seeking out other kids who are exploring gender, rather than being influenced by them. Also, adolescence is a time of experimentation. Kids are trying out different friends and activities and clothing choices. From my perspective, gender exploration isn't a problem, even if they change a few times—like trying out soccer, then switching to marching band, and then debate club. Sometimes, that's how they know what fits for them.

Celine: I understand the points you're making. I just have a different view. I don't think it's healthy for kids to "experiment" with something as fundamental as gender, but I can see how it wouldn't seem like a problem to you if you don't see gender the way I do.

Kevin: I hear you. Yes, we do seem to have different views about gender. From my perspective, I don't think it's healthy for kids to be confined to a gender that doesn't fit for them.

Celine: Yeah, thank you for weighing in and helping me see another side of the issue. I have a better sense of where you're coming from.

Kevin: I'm glad you sought out my opinion and shared yours.

You might notice that Kevin and Celine both had strong views, but they spoke about their views as being their own opinions, not as moral or rational truths. Celine exemplified intellectual humility by reaching out to Kevin to hear a different view from her own, and Kevin responded with intellectual humility by demonstrating respect and curiosity.

IN SUM

This chapter has helped you identify ways that you might cultivate understanding of people who differ from you politically.

First, recognizing that your views of others are likely distorted may open you to shifting your understanding and may help motivate you to do so. Generating warm feelings toward others may create a positive foundation for dialogue. Perspective taking can be both a precursor and an outcome of dialogue. Both within and beyond dialogue, you can gain a deeper understanding of people who differ from you. All of these approaches will help to move beyond distortions, stereotypes, and limited perspective to bring others into clearer focus, providing a solid foundation for dialogue.

Now that you've got the skills to hear and take the perspective of others, let's get you talking, too.

NOTES

1. Robinson, R. J., Keltner, D., Ward, A., & Ross, L. (1995). Actual versus assumed differences in construal: "Naive realism" in intergroup perception and conflict. *Journal of Personality and Social Psychology, 68,* 404. https://doi.org/10.1037/0022-3514.68.3.404
2. Westfall, J., Van Boven, L., Chambers, J. R., & Judd, C. M. (2015). Perceiving political polarization in the United States: Party identity strength and attitude extremity exacerbate the perceived partisan divide. *Perspectives on Psychological Science, 10,* 145–158. https://doi.org/10.1177/1745691615569849
3. Hawkins, S., Yudkin, D., Juan-Torres, M., & Dixon, T. (2018). *Hidden tribes: A study of America's polarized landscape.* https://hiddentribes.us/midterms-update
4. Waytz, A., Young, L. L., & Ginges, J. (2014). Motive attribution asymmetry for love vs hate drive intractable conflict. *PNAS, 111,* 15687–15692. https://doi.org/10.1073/pnas.1414146111
5. Gehlbach, H. (2004). A new perspective on perspective taking: A multidimensional approach to conceptualizing an aptitude. *Educational Psychology Review, 16,* 207–234.

6. Gehlbach, H., & Brinkworth, M. E. (2012). The social perspective taking process: Strategies and sources of evidence in taking another's perspective. *Teachers College Record, 114*, 226–254.

7. I am grateful to Professor Hunter Gehlbach for sharing with me an activity that this exercise is based on.

8. Vance, J. D. (2016). *Hillbilly elegy: A memoir of a family and culture in crisis.* Harper Collins Publishers.

9. Hochschild, A. R. (2018). *Strangers in their own land: Anger and mourning on the American Right.* The New Press.

10. Haidt, J. (2012). *The righteous mind: Why good people are divided by politics and religion.* Pantheon Books.

11. Weber, C. R., & Federico, C. M. (2013). Moral foundations and heterogeneity in ideological preference. *Political Psychology, 34*, 107–126. https://doi.org/10.1111/j.1467-9221.2012.00922.x

12. Feinberg, M., & Willer, R. (2015). From gulf to bridge: When do moral arguments facilitate political influence? *Personality and Social Psychology Bulletin, 41*(12), 1665–1681. https://doi.org/10.1177/0146167215607842

13. Cardwell, M. (1999). *Dictionary of psychology.* Fitzroy Dearborn.

14. Adichie, C. N. (2009, July). *The danger of a single story* [Video]. TEDGlobal Conference. https://www.ted.com/talks/chimamanda_ngozi_adichie_the_danger_of_a_single_story/transcript

15. https://en.wikipedia.org/wiki/Righteousness

16. https://en.wikipedia.org/wiki/Self-righteousness

17. Van Tongeren, D. R., Stafford, J., Hook, J. N., Green, J. D., Davis, D. E., & Johnson, K. A. (2016). Humility attenuates negative attitudes and behaviors toward religious out-group members. *The Journal of Positive Psychology, 11*, 199–208. https://doi.org/10.1080/17439760.2015.1037861

18. Woodruff, E., Van Tongeren, D. R., McElroy, S., Davis, D. E., & Hook, J. N. (2014). Humility and religion: Benefits, difficulties, and a model of religious tolerance. In *Religion and spirituality across cultures* (p. 280). Springer.

19. Lynch, M. P., Johnson, C. R., Sheff, N., & Gunn, H. (n.d.). *Intellectual humility in public discourse.* https://humilityandconviction.uconn.edu/blank/what-is-intellectual-humility

20. Leary, M. R., Diebels, K. J., Davisson, E. K., Jongman-Sereno, K. P., Isherwood, J. C., Raimi, K. T., Deffler, S. A., & Hoyle, R. H. (2017). Cognitive and interpersonal features of intellectual humility. *Personality and Social Psychology Bulletin, 43*, 793–813. https://doi.org/10.1177/0146167217697695

21. Porter, T., & Schumann, K. (2018). Intellectual humility and openness to the opposing view. *Self and Identity, 17*, 139–162. https://doi.org/10.1080/15298868.2017.1361861

22. Dweck, Carol S. (2008) *Mindset: The new psychology of success.* Ballantine Books.

23. Van Tongeren, D. R., Stafford, J., Hook, J. N., Green, J. D., Davis, D. E., & Johnson, K. A. (2016). Humility attenuates negative attitudes and behaviors toward religious out-group members. *The Journal of Positive Psychology, 11*, 199–208. https://doi.org/10.1080/17439760.2015.1037861

CHAPTER 6

TALKING SKILLS

DO I FINALLY GET TO SPEAK?

In the past several chapters, you've read about how to listen, manage your emotions, and understand others. You may be wondering, "When do I actually get to speak?" Perhaps you feel impatient picturing yourself simply listening, reflecting, breathing, and trying to recall someone's positive qualities. Maybe imagining keeping your views to yourself while you subject yourself to endless elaboration on opinions you disagree with makes you want to tear your hair out. Never fear, this chapter will offer guidance about how to speak effectively for purposes of sharing your views, persuasion, and finding common ground.

Before moving into talking, I want to remind you that the preceding chapters provide an important foundation for speaking. It's been said: Nobody cares how much you know, until they know how much you care (a quote often attributed to Teddy Roosevelt). The listening skills described in Chapter 3 help to demonstrate that you care what someone else has to say and makes it more likely that they will want to hear your perspective. Managing your emotions (Chapter 4) puts you in a better place to be able to express yourself and helps others hear what you have to say. Understanding others (Chapter 5) can help you frame what you want to say in a way that it may be embraced by them. So if you skipped over those chapters, I encourage you to go back and read them. Indeed, you may find that after you've mastered the skills presented earlier in this book, talking may be unnecessary, or at least less significant than you might have originally thought, to achieve your goals for dialogue.

TELLING YOUR STORY

Read these four narratives and note your reactions to them:

> *Erica:* I'm an environmentalist because I care about the future of our planet and want to protect it for the next generation. Fuel emissions release CO_2 into the atmosphere, which contributes to global warming. This is why we're having more severe weather, including droughts, fires, and hurricanes. We should be investing in petroleum-free technology, like electric cars. People who support the use of fossil fuel are ignoring science. Scientists agree that human beings are causing climate change, and human beings can stop it. But if we don't act now, it will be too late.
>
> *Owen:* The fact is, Americans drive a lot of cars, and we need oil to run them. If we want to be independent of Arab nations for our oil, we need to drill for oil that's on our own land. Natural resources in public areas are just that, a resource, and we should be making use of the resources available on our land. Oil drilling also provides jobs in the

U.S. I can't understand why environmentalists are trying to shut down oil drilling—it sounds crazy to me. Why would we want to leave perfectly good oil in the ground instead of using it?

Maria: I grew up in an area with a lot of oil drilling. Most of my friends' parents worked in some aspect of oil production. Oil was an integral part of our town. In fact, I remember the sense of pride I felt when I got my first car and filled it up at the gas station—I felt like I was supporting my community. I never worked in oil, but I have the utmost respect for my friends who do—they're good people who have great admiration for the land and the resources it provides. That's why I think it's important to protect the oil industry from overregulation.

Victor: When I was a kid, my family went camping every summer. I loved those vacations, exploring, fishing, hiking. Growing up in a city, I was awed by the peace and beauty of nature. As an adult, I introduced my children to hiking and camping at an early age, and we really bonded as a family during these times. I started to think about how much I wanted to preserve the opportunities to explore nature for my children, and eventually, grandchildren. That's what led me to the environmental movement.

I suspect your reactions to the narratives differed somewhat on the basis of your opinions about environmentalism and oil. If you're more supportive of environmentalism, you might notice yourself nodding in agreement with Erica and Victor, and you might need to practice managing your emotions when you read Owen's and Maria's narratives.

But there are not only different positions represented; there are different communication approaches, as well. Consider your reactions to Erica and Owen compared with Maria and Victor. If you found yourself wanting to argue some of Owen's or Erica's points and curious to hear more from Victor and Maria, that's no surprise.

Owen and Erica offered logical arguments based on factual information. But the arguments we make to support our views are likely not the *reasons* we hold those views, at least not in isolation from our values and life experience. The problem is not that our facts are inaccurate, it's that they're insignificant without the context of how we came to form these views in the first place.

Another problem with Erica's and Owen's approach is what they imply about people who disagree with them. Erica says people who support oil use don't believe in science. Owen suggests that it's crazy not to support oil. These implications about those who hold opposing views are subtly aggressive and can provoke discord, thereby derailing dialogue. It's important to notice the assumptions about other people embedded in what we say. For example, "I support charter schools because I care about children" implies that people who don't support charter schools don't care about children. Notice how you might be jabbing at someone else based on what you say about your own views.

Maria and Victor used a storytelling approach. They shared how they came to form their views within the contexts of their own lives. Storytelling invites another person along on your journey of forming the views you hold. This can help them understand the richness of your position. It may also help move someone closer to your view if they relate to the path you've described.

You might notice that when you share your story, you feel some sense of vulnerability. When you share your story, you're opening yourself up to another person, and you don't know how they'll react. It might feel easier to share factual information and abstract arguments because they're less personal, but they're also less effective. If you're nervous about opening yourself up in this way, it may be helpful to practice sharing your stories with others whose opinions are similar to your own. Ask how they came to hold their views and share your own. This is another great opportunity to practice listening, reflecting, and asking open-ended questions.

Have you ever been in a group of people where some folks will share their views and others will agree, but a few will be silent? When we assume others hold the same opinions we do, we might unintentionally alienate some people in group conversations. An advantage of the storytelling approach is that it offers a way to have conversations

What's Your Story?

Instructions: This activity is an opportunity for you to articulate your story about an issue. I suggest you try writing your story. You can either answer each question, or you can write in whatever form suits you, trying to touch on each of the questions.

1. Think of an issue that you have an opinion about and that you might like to discuss with someone who holds a different opinion.
2. What opinions about this issue do you recall hearing from family, friends, teachers, faith leaders, media, or others?
3. What aspects of your values or experience relate to this issue?
4. When do you first recall having your own opinion about this issue? What was the context in which you originally formed or stated this opinion?
5. How has your opinion shifted or deepened or remained the same over time?

in groups with mixed views without alienating or silencing people. Even if it turns out everyone has similar opinions, storytelling may promote meaningful conversation instead of everyone simply making the same arguments and nodding their heads. Although we may come to the same conclusions, our stories are unique.

BRIDGING THE DIVIDE

You may recall from Chapter 5 that your perceptions of those whom you disagree with might be distorted and that you might be overestimating the distance between your views and theirs. But the research I've shared also reveals an actual difference in views that has increased over time. Is there a way to decrease polarization? The answer is yes, but first let me tell you what *not* to do.

One study found a way to make us even more polarized than we actually are.[1] How could we increase polarization? First, we would find Republicans and Democrats who use Twitter; we would then send liberal tweets to the Republicans and conservative tweets to the Democrats. If we did that, then what we might find is that the more they paid attention to those tweets, the more polarized they would become. In other words, the more Democrats looked at conservative tweets, the more liberal they would become, and the more Republicans read liberal tweets, the more conservative they would become. (The effect on Republicans would be even more potent than the effect on Democrats, according to this study.) Basically, if you want to temper the extremities of people's views, oppositional tweeting is not the road to success!

If we want to reduce polarization, we need to address human tendencies that contribute to extreme views. For example, we often *don't know what we don't know*, and we think we understand things better than we do.[2] Furthermore, we strengthen our existing views through confirmation bias, selectively seeking information and processing it in ways that are consistent with the way we already see things.[3,4] So the same information is going to be viewed differently by different people. We also typically connect with other people who hold similar views.[5]

Explaining Your Position

A group of researchers created an experiment to see if they could combat these human tendencies that keep us inside our own bubbles.[6] Let's try it!

1. First, indicate your position on these policies by rating them on a scale of 1 (*strongly against*) to 7 (*strongly in favor*):
   a. Eliminating the death penalty
   b. Requiring abstinence-only sex education
2. Next, rate how well you understand each issue, from 1 (*vague understanding*) to 7 (*thorough understanding*):
   a. Eliminating the death penalty
   b. Requiring abstinence-only sex education
3. Please describe all the details you know about each policy, going from the first step to the last, and stating precisely how each step causes the next step. Take your time and try to be as complete as possible.
4. Again, indicate your position on these policies by rating them on a scale of 1 (*strongly against*) to 7 (*strongly in favor*):
   a. Eliminating the death penalty
   b. Requiring abstinence-only sex education
5. Again, rate how well you understand each issue, from 1 (*vague understanding*) to 7 (*thorough understanding*):
   a. Eliminating the death penalty
   b. Requiring abstinence-only sex education

What we would likely find is that if you held an extreme view to begin with, after providing the sort of *mechanistic explanation* elicited here, your position would have become more moderate and you would rate your understanding as lower than your initial rating. In contrast, if you have been asked to explain why you support the position instead of explicating the policy, your ratings would not change at all.

This experiment highlights the *illusion of explanatory depth*,[7] which describes our tendency to believe that we understand phenomena better than we actually do. Providing information that contrasts with our understanding or asking us why we hold the positions we do does not seem to change our beliefs about our understanding. However, asking for a mechanistic explanation may help people assess their own comprehension with greater accuracy. Thus, asking someone to elaborate on their position may help them to recognize the limits of their understanding more than challenging their views with contrasting information. One caveat is that the experiment was done in an online environment, so it is not entirely clear how it would work in a face-to-face setting where people may feel challenged to defend their position.

COMMON GROUND WITH KEVIN AND CELINE

Are you motivated to participate in dialogue across political lines to find common ground? This desire to connect and acknowledge shared interests is one I hear frequently. The good news is, there may be more common ground than you imagine. In Chapter 5, you read that people tend to overestimate the differences between their own views and those of political opponents so there's likely less distance to bridge than you think. In addition, contact with people who aren't like yourself may help correct biased judgments:[8] they may be more reasonable and likeable than you anticipate.

Let's consider potential areas for common ground. Are there areas of policy you can agree on? One of the challenges with this is the illusion of explanatory depth, described earlier. Most people don't understand policy on a detailed level, and those who do may not agree with each other on policy analysis, legal precedent, or public opinion. Consider, for example, Celine and Kevin talking about abortion.

Kevin: A majority of the American public supports a woman's right to choose, so it seems like we should be able to find some agreement here.

Celine: But a majority of the American public says they want some restrictions on late-term abortions, so maybe we can agree on that.

Kevin: But late-term abortions are done very infrequently, typically only to save the life of the mother.

Celine: So why not put that into the law?

Kevin: Well, it's a slippery slope. Once we say these decisions can be made by the state rather than by a woman and her doctor, we've taken it out of the realm of a medical decision and made it a political one.

Celine: No, we've made it an ethical one. We want laws that support ethical behavior, so we don't want people to be able to terminate a pregnancy when the child could live outside the mother. Neonatal medicine has made a lot of advances, and we can save these children's lives earlier and earlier in the pregnancy, so why not give the child the chance to live?

You can see that Kevin and Celine both have factual information and legal analysis that they're bringing into the conversation, but it doesn't seem to help them find common ground. Here are some suggestions that may help when you're trying to bridge the divide. First, find at least one point of the other side's argument that you think has some legitimacy and acknowledge your agreement with it. Here's what that might look like:

> *Kevin:* A majority of the American public supports a woman's right to choose, so it seems like we should be able to find some agreement here.
>
> *Celine:* Yes, I've seen that, and I think it's important to pay attention to people's opinions. I've also seen polls saying that a majority of the American public expresses they want some restrictions on late-term abortions, so maybe we can agree on that.
>
> *Kevin:* It's true, I can understand why people feel uncomfortable with late-term abortions. Fortunately, late-term abortions are done very infrequently, typically only to save the life of the mother.

You can see here that both Celine and Kevin could find something they agreed with in what the other was saying. It may be more challenging to do this than it appears. You might feel like conceding any point in the argument weakens your position, which could make you reluctant to affirm any aspect of the other person's views, even if you agree. If you're motivated by finding common ground, it may be helpful to keep your goal in mind and remember that acknowledging something the other person said can help you achieve your goal.

It's important to be flexible regarding the type of ground you might have in common. When you don't find intersections where you hoped to, consider other possible areas for connection. The similarities you find may not be directly related to policies or issues you care most passionately about. Perhaps you think, "Even though we don't agree on abortion, I'm sure we will both want to reduce pregnancies by making contraception more widely available." This is a very specific and predetermined outcome. Instead, you could start by trying to find shared personal hopes, fears, goals, interests, likes, dislikes, and experiences. Maybe you discover that you both enjoy Blueberry Pop Tarts or watching *Scandal* or playing tennis. These surface similarities may not feel as satisfying as solving the federal deficit, but even a small win can be meaningful when you're trying to connect across the political divide.

If you do get to the point of talking about specific issues, you can try telling your stories as described earlier in this chapter. You might also look for shared values, even if they're related to different views. For example, I've been thinking about what's behind the positions people take on guns and abortion. There are people who are pro-life, and there are people who are for gun control, and they are often different people; however, they have some things in common on the level of underlying values. Both the arguments for restricting abortion and the arguments for restricting guns are about protecting life, especially children's lives. Of course, pro-life people don't necessarily agree that limiting access to assault rifles will save children's lives, and gun control advocates don't necessarily think restricting abortion is about saving babies. Nonetheless, both sides are willing to give up some freedom in the name of protecting children. Pro-life people are willing to give up access to abortion, and gun control advocates are willing to give up the right to own a gun. This may be a challenging conversation to have because there may be contrasting conclusions related to the shared values, but if you're really committed to common ground, you may need to let go of your impulse to focus on the points of disagreement, at least initially.

Finally, you might need to agree to disagree on some points. As much as you want to find common ground, it's important to be flexible and realistic in your expectations. Find connections where you can, and be prepared to let it go if your efforts are not fruitful.

PERSUASION

What if your primary motivation is to change someone's mind, to bridge the divide by bringing them closer to your view? You might be wondering if it's even possible to enter into dialogue with the goal of persuasion, or if the desire to convince or convert will necessarily undermine the connection. I admit that it's a challenging undertaking with numerous potential pitfalls. It's particularly important to have a realistic idea of what persuasion looks like and to keep in mind that it is not always the same thing as expressing your views. With that in mind, what's the best way to persuade someone to embrace your perspective or to act or vote in a particular way?

First, reflect on your motives: Why do you want to change their mind? One of the most tangible reasons to care about someone's views is that you're invested in the outcome of an election (for example, as a candidate or canvasser), and you're speaking to them as a voter. But what if that's not the reason, or at least not the whole picture? Do you have any underlying investment in their views? Perhaps you're feeling frustrated that someone does not believe the information your opinion is based on. Maybe you worry that they're being manipulated by "fake news" or political rhetoric. Possibly you feel like their beliefs disregard your values or experiences or well-being. It's important to know what's driving you, as this insight can help you to make thoughtful choices about whether and how you approach persuasion attempts.

Once you understand your own motives, it is helpful to understand the other person in the context of persuasion: What moves someone to be persuaded? On the basis of psychological research, Robert Cialdini has articulated six principles of persuasion, and he's aptly applied them to situations in which the goal is to gain compliance in business and other situations.[9] The good news is that these principles can be applied to political dialogue, and you've already learned about some of these. For example, *reciprocity* can be helpful when seeking common ground: If you acknowledge the legitimacy of some aspect of the other person's argument, they may feel some obligation to accept something you say. Also, *liking* is associated with successful persuasion, so you may be more successful in shifting someone's views if you communicate warmth and caring through listening; identify similarities between yourself and the other person (as discussed regarding common ground), and become more familiar through positive interactions—all of which you've already learned about in this book!

Let's consider how Cialdini's remaining principles might apply to persuasion regarding political issues:

- *Consistency* refers to people's tendency to act in ways that are consistent with their prior actions or views of themselves. Although consistency might stand in the way of persuasion by leading someone to stick to their existing beliefs, it may provide an avenue for shifting someone's views if you can frame the new perspective as consistent with their commitments, behaviors, or self-image.
- Furthermore, people tend to act in ways that are consistent with other people's behaviors, and they seek *social proof* to align themselves with their peers. Thus, providing evidence that the position you support is endorsed by most people may be helpful.
- Also important, though, is providing information from a source that the other person would see as credible and expert—*authority* isn't effective if not accepted as legitimate by the recipient.

- Cialdini's final principle of *scarcity* suggests that arousal generated by time limitations can push someone toward a specific behavior. This may not be applicable to shifting political views, but it may help motivate action on views. If you are trying to persuade someone to vote, for example, a reminder that this is the final opportunity to make a difference in the outcome may move them to act.

Even using these principles, impediments to persuasion make it difficult to change someone's mind. First, keep in mind that people respond to factual information through a lens of *confirmation bias.* This means that they tend to believe information that supports their existing views and dismiss information contrary to what they think is true. This tendency is true for people on both sides of the political divide, even though naïve realism may be at play, such that we are certain our own beliefs are based in fact but that others are swayed by political rhetoric (see Chapter 5 for more on naïve realism). Keeping these tendencies in mind may rein in your desire to overwhelm the other person with a barrage of factual information. It may also keep you from questioning the intelligence of anyone who disagrees with you. (Much of the research on confirmation bias has been conducted with college students, so it's clear that even educated people are susceptible to unconscious psychological processes.)

Next, if you're trying to persuade someone, it's important to treat them with respect. Ideally, the material in Chapter 5 has helped you perceive them more clearly and understand their perspective. With these foundational insights, you may be able to help them feel understood by listening and reflecting their views accurately (see Chapter 3). Being respectful also means not dismissing their views, values, or experiences. Keep in mind that they may have moral priorities different from your own, so you should assume that their views are guided by morality. Consider your tone as well. Notice if you sound judgmental or condescending, and try to shift to communicate warmth and respect. Antagonism does not change minds, so a calm demeanor is key (see Chapter 4).

When trying to change someone's mind, you may be tempted to point out logical inconsistencies in their arguments. One of the best places to find people doing this is on Twitter. Try selecting a politically divisive hashtag, and you are likely to find people on both sides of the issue pointing out problems with the arguments posed by the other side. When I view these allegations through a neutral lens, I have to admit, they're not wrong. I can see how each side can identify inconsistencies or illogic of the other side. Nonetheless, these "gotchas" are disrespectful, and they are also not an effective approach to persuasion.

Confronting someone with factual information or opinions that conflict with their existing views may cause them to dig their heels into their position.[10] So what alternative strategies might be persuasive? Earlier in this chapter, you were introduced to the *mechanistic explanation*, which consists of describing how something works, step by step. Providing mechanistic explanations makes people less polarized in their views and more humble in their assessment of their understanding of policies. In dialogue, this might be accomplished by asking for elaboration. For example, if someone suggests that voting should be mandatory, you could respond, "I'd like to hear more about that. Can you explain how that would work?" It would be important to ask with genuine curiosity and to follow up with active listening, including reflection.

You may recall that the alternative to the mechanistic explanation was asking people to articulate the reasons why they support a particular position, and this did nothing to shift people's views. Yet this is typically what we elicit from people when we challenge their views—they share the reasons and rationale, which may do nothing but reinforce their existing stance. This is why dialogue has greater potential to change minds than debate does.

Perhaps the most useful guidance I can offer about persuasion is to have realistic expectations of your power to shift someone's views. Success may be incremental and require prolonged contact, or it may not happen at all. Your success will be limited by the numerous motives and mechanisms for resisting persuasion.[11] Skills and strategies in this book—listening, managing emotions, understanding others, telling your story—are the best possible preparation for you to bring someone closer to your position. If, however, you sacrifice these foundations of dialogue in your interactions, you have little chance of being persuasive. Focus on the relationship, and persuasion may follow.

In this chapter, you learned the positive effect of telling your story and tips for engaging in persuasive dialogue. You learned about barriers to bridging the divide and how to find ways toward common ground, even if they don't relate to a political issue. In the next chapter, we'll look at the dynamic between you and your dialogue partners and learn to how to consciously negotiate disparities.

NOTES

1. Bail, C. A., Argyle, L. P., Brown, T. W., Bumpus, J. P., Chen, H., Hunzaker, M. B. F., Lee, J., Mann, M., Merhout, F., & Volfovsky, A. (2018). Exposure to opposing views can increase political polarization: Evidence from a large-scale field experiment on social media. *PNAS, 37*, 9216–9221. https://doi.org/10.1073/pnas.1804840115

2. Kruger, J., & Dunning, D. (1999). Unskilled and unaware of it: How difficulties in recognizing one's own incompetence lead to inflated self-assessments. *Journal of Personality and Social Psychology, 77*(6), 1121–1134. https://doi.org/10.1037/0022-3514.77.6.1121

3. Lord, C. G., Ross, L., & Lepper, M. R. (1979). Biased assimilation and attitude polarization: The effects of prior theories on sub-

sequently considered evidence. *Journal of Personality and Social Psychology*, *37*(11), 2098–2109. https://doi.org/10.1037/0022-3514.37.11.2098

4. Nickerson, R. S. (1998). Confirmation bias: A ubiquitous phenomenon in many guises. *Review of General Psychology*, *2*(2), 175–220. https://doi.org/10.1037/1089-2680.2.2.175

5. Lazarsfeld, P. F., & Merton, R. K. (1954). Friendship as a social process: A substantive and methodological analysis. *Freedom and Control in Modern Society*, *18*(1), 18–66.

6. Fernbach, P. M., Rogers, T., Fox, C. R., & Sloman, S. A. (2013). Political extremism is supported by an illusion of understanding. *Psychological Science*, *24*(6), 939–946. https://doi.org/10.1177/0956797612464058

7. Rozenblit, L., & Keil, F. (2002). The misunderstood limits of folk science: An illusion of explanatory depth. *Cognitive Science*, *26*(5), 521–562. https://doi.org/10.1016/S0364-0213(02)00078-2

8. Allport, G. W., & Kramer, B. M. (1946). Some roots of prejudice. *The Journal of Psychology: Interdisciplinary and Applied*, *22*(1), 9–39. https://doi.org/10.1080/00223980.1946.9917293

9. Cialdini, R. B. (2006). *Influence: The psychology of persuasion* (Rev. ed.). Harper Business.

10. Hart, P. S., & Nisbet, E. C. (2012). Boomerang effects in science communication: How motivated reasoning and identity cues amplify opinion polarization about climate mitigation policies. *Communication Research*, *39*(6), 701–723. https://doi.org/10.1177/0093650211416646

11. Fransen, M. L., Smit, E. G., & Verlegh, P. W. (2015). Strategies and motives for resistance to persuasion: An integrative framework. *Frontiers in Psychology*, *6*, 1201. https://doi.org/10.3389/fpsyg.2015.01201

CHAPTER 7

DIALOGUE SKILLS IN CONTEXT

I hope that, by this point in the book, you've developed an appreciation for the skills that can support dialogue across political lines. Do these skills automatically lead to successful dialogue in every situation? Will both parties remain calm, respectful, and invested in understanding each other and bridging the divide? Not necessarily. Listening, managing emotions, understanding others, and talking effectively are key ingredients, but they may operate differently depending on the dynamics between yourself and your dialogue partner.

HOW INVESTED ARE YOU IN THE RELATIONSHIP?

Dialogue dynamics depend on your history with your dialogue partner. There may be occasions where you strike up a conversation with someone you don't know—waiting for a bus, socializing at a bar, seated next to you at a baseball game—and it becomes apparent that there's a difference in political views. You have a choice in these situations whether you will continue the conversation or end it. With a stranger, you have very little investment. Your relationship can end when the bus comes, when you leave the bar, or after the ninth inning. In some ways, this is an ideal situation in which to hone your dialogue skills since you have nothing to lose if things don't go well. As enthusiastic as I am for dialogue across political lines, I must admit that sometimes I pass up these opportunities simply because I don't have energy to spare or I want to focus my attention on other matters. Also, you don't know whether the other person wants to engage in dialogue, so it's best to start with listening, managing emotions, and trying to understand. Only if they seem interested in your views should you move to sharing your own perspectives.

Consider people in your community, with whom you may not be close but see on a regular basis—coworkers, members of your faith community, and your children's friends' parents, for instance. You can choose, or choose not, to deepen your relationship through dialogue. Some communities are encouraging dialogue because there may be tension or some people may feel alienated when they perceive the majority to hold a view that's different from their own. So, there may not be an individual payoff as much as a community benefit to engaging in these conversations.

You might find yourself with someone you don't know, but in a more intentional context in which the goal is to have dialogue about politics. Maybe, for example, you're inspired to join a group that has the goal of bridging the political divide through dialogue (see the Additional Resources section at the end of the book for information on some of these initiatives) or perhaps you're involved in a campaign and going door-to-door advocating for an issue or a candidate. In these situations, you and the other person both know what your purpose is. So, although you don't have a prior or ongoing relationship, you've already committed to the dialogue, and the other person has made a conscious choice about whether to participate.

The most fraught situations I hear about involve a meaningful and ongoing relationship that is affected by political discord. When the conflict is with family members or close friends, both parties are invested in the relationship but not necessarily open to dialogue. Throughout this book, you've witnessed Celine and Kevin grappling with dialogue as an example of family members interested in reducing their political conflict. See also Chapter 2 for suggestions for inviting someone into dialogue, but keep in mind that not everyone will want to participate. At the beginning of this book, I framed the material as applying to dialogue *with someone who wants to be in dialogue*. It is unlikely that you will accomplish your goals if you drag your dialogue partner in kicking and screaming.

SKILLFULNESS IN DIALOGUE

We are not born with the skills that contribute to successful dialogue, so we need help developing them. Some people seem to pick up them more easily than others, so even if both parties in a dialogue have been exposed to dialogue skills, they may not implement them flawlessly, and there may be some disparity in the skill level of the dialogue partners.

It's helpful if you try your best while attempting to accept imperfection—in yourself and your partner. No one wants to be told they're doing things wrong all the time, so try to be forgiving if your dialogue partner doesn't reflect what you're saying accurately or if you get a little ruffled. At the same time, you'll need to decide what level of skills you both need to be able to engage in a constructive dialogue. If your dialogue partner hasn't read this book or been exposed to these skills in another way, you may need to determine what level of emotional reactivity, interrupting, and one-sided sharing of their own views you can withstand. You may be able to shift or encourage their dialogue skills through modeling and the types of questions you ask, but be prepared for a potential skill imbalance.

DISTANCE BETWEEN VIEWS

Keep in mind that for dialogue to occur, the other person does not need to be at the opposite extreme of the political spectrum from yourself. In fact, some of the most heated conflicts occur among people who have similar goals but different visions for how to achieve them. These tools will work well for dialogue with people who are closer to your views but who are not exactly on the same page. For example, Republicans could apply these skills for conversations about what conservatism means, Democrats could reflect on Bernie versus Hillary, or incremental versus systemic change, voters can talk with nonvoters, and those who are affiliated with political parties could engage with people who are Independents.

THE POLITICS OF PIZZA

Other things may affect dialogue dynamics, including culture, power, and personality. I'll try to illuminate these matters through an experience that you may have had: sharing a pizza. For the purposes of this analogy, we'll need to assume that you have to get the same thing on the whole pizza—no half Hawaiian and half mushroom. Why? Because you share one common dialogue experience with another person. You may come at it from different perspectives, and the way it plays out and any common ground you arrive at require negotiation.

Let's say Celine and Kevin are ordering a pizza, and they both want sausage and peppers. This would be the equivalent of having dialogue with someone who agrees with you on everything. It's easy, and everyone gets what they want.

But what if Celine wants sausage and peppers, and Kevin wants artichoke hearts and garlic? This is like dialogue across political lines. If they're respectful of each other and have mastered dialogue skills, they might each say what they want while the other listens and then seek common ground. If neither of them can persuade the other, they might end up with a cheese pizza—not exactly what either wants, but they can both live with it. They might disagree, but there's no judgment about what the other wants—it's simply a matter of preference.

What if Celine and Kevin's pizza topping choices are based in their values or lifestyles? Kevin wants soy cheese because he's vegan—he's done a lot of research about how animals are mistreated in factory farms, and he made a life choice not to use animal products. On the other hand, Celine is a dairy farmer. She hears Kevin's position as a criticism—she feels like he's saying her livelihood and way of life are harmful, although she feels like her work helps to sustain her family and other families who rely on milk products. This is more typical of dialogue across political lines. The positions are not simply opinions; rather, they are connected to deeply held beliefs, and they have tangible consequences for people's lives.

How might culture and tradition play into the equation? Consider the possibility that Celine's husband's family is from Italy, and they're very connected to their Italian heritage, including thin crust pizza. Kevin's wife is a New Yorker who grew up on Ray's pizza with substantial crust with lots of toppings. Here choice of crust is about dedication to family and upbringing. Each gravitates toward the pizza crust that is familiar and comforting, the alternative seeming alien and certainly not appetizing. Political positions are formed in the context of culture, tradition, and family. When views clash, another viewpoint is not neutral; it is foreign and unwelcome.

In these examples so far, there are equally justifiable reasons on both sides. What happens when the outcome has more severe consequences for one person than the other—does each party's perspective have the same weight? Let's say Celine has celiac disease—eating gluten can result in damage to her intestine. Kevin feels like the "gluten-free craze" has gotten out of hand. When the decision affects one party's well-being, are all choices equally valid? In dialogue, it's worth considering the personal stake of each party in the issue—what do they have to lose? Of course, in the political realm, both sides may feel like their position represents those who are most vulnerable.

How might a disparity in resources affect the pizza negotiation? If Kevin doesn't have money to contribute to the pizza, and Celine is paying the full price, do they both have a say in what kind of pizza to get? Power may come into play in dialogue, as well if one party is in a position of authority over the other, such as a parent–child or employer–employee pairing. The person with less power may not be comfortable expressing their views, may feel pressure to agree with their superior, and may not feel like they have the choice about whether to engage in dialogue in the first place. This can occur even when there isn't a concrete hierarchical relationship simply because people experience the relationship as imbalanced. Inequities in perceived power could be due to economic differences, identities (such as gender, ethnicity, or sexual orientation), or prior experiences, such as trauma. You may not even be aware that your dialogue partner is feeling powerless. It's important not to pressure others to join you in dialogue because they might feel coerced. Applying the skills of listening, managing emotions, and understanding can help you to be attuned to the experiences and feelings of dialogue partners and create a more comfortable environment for their participation in dialogue. If you're feeling vulnerable, you may be more likely to experience the fight–flight–freeze response than if you were in power. It's important to assess your safety and determine whether you're feeling a sense of threat due to powerlessness or if you really are in danger. If you choose to stay in dialogue, you can draw on the skills in Chapter 4 to manage the emotions that arise.

As you can see, even the simplest negotiation, such as pizza toppings, can be complex. Dialogue across political lines is riddled with these sorts of challenges—values, lifestyle, culture, tradition, consequences, and power. Use of dialogue skills can help to promote constructive conversation, but keep in mind that there may be more subtle dynamics than are immediately apparent from what you see and hear on the surface.

IDENTITIES AND AFFILIATIONS WITH CELINE AND KEVIN

Although we may frame the political in contrast to the personal, they are intertwined. Politics is often about policies that are rooted in our values and experiences and that have a tangible impact on our lives. Let's consider these complexities as Celine and Kevin describe their views about police use of force and Black Lives Matter.

> *Celine:* I'm so upset about these Black Lives Matter people. I mean, how can they say other people are racist when they're so focused on race—"Black lives matter." Don't all lives matter? What about the lives of the police? They're putting themselves in danger every day to protect us all. You know, when something happens in our community, and everyone's running away, police are running toward it. They have to approach every situation as if it's potentially lethal, because it might be. We should be thanking them, and they're being portrayed as racists who are just out to get Black people. It used to be a respected profession, and now no one wants to be a cop anymore.
>
> *Kevin:* It seems like every week another unarmed Black man is shot by police. These men were just

minding their own business—driving to work, playing in their own neighborhood. Sure, some had minor violations—driving with a broken taillight—how many people do that? But White people don't get shot for it. And then there are no consequences for the cops. They say they felt threatened—there's a big difference between feeling threatened and actually being threatened. If you feel threatened only by Black people, maybe you have biases you're not even aware of, and then you shouldn't be allowed to have a gun and a badge. It's frustrating and frightening that the people who are supposed to protect everyone are killing innocent people.

How did it feel for you to read these perspectives? How might your opinions and reactions be influenced by your own experiences with police or with race or by the views of people in your family and community? What assumptions might you have about people who express sentiments similar to Celine's and Kevin's?

What would it be like for Kevin and Celine to have dialogue about this issue? It would be important for them to recognize their biases—not only about people who hold these views but also any responses they have to each other's characteristics, such as ethnic background, education level, and accent.

What if Celine and Kevin have a conversation in which they tell their stories, listen with respect, and seek common ground? They may have friends and family with whom they feel connected due to shared values about the issues, as well as shared views about people on the other side. Engaging in respectful dialogue with someone on the other side may put Kevin and Celine in conflict with the people who agree with them on the issues, but who would see dialogue with someone who disagrees as compromising values or selling out.

Dialogue does not take place in a vacuum. Our opinions have been shaped by our experiences and values and in the context of our identities and affiliations. These contexts can support our views, sometimes shielding us from contrasting information and perspectives. Engaging in dialogue may shift our understanding, unmoor our certainty, and open us to new ways of thinking. Consider how you will navigate dialogue's potential ripple effect on your relationships, identity, and community.

In the next chapter, I'll offer some final thoughts before you put these skills into action.

CHAPTER 8

DIALOGUE SKILLS IN ACTION

At this point, you've learned how to *listen*, *talk*, *manage your emotions*, and *understand others*. You've had opportunities to reflect on your motivations, practice skills, and to review examples. You have everything you need to engage in dialogue. In this chapter, I offer some final thoughts on assessing your readiness for dialogue, and addresses barriers that may be keeping you from dialogue. I provide suggestions for how to bring your political conversations to an end. I close the chapter with a discussion of two themes that underlie many of the recommendations offered in this book: integrity and grace.

STRENGTHENING DIALOGUE SKILLS

Consider preparation for dialogue as strength training. What if you wanted to be able to lift 80 pounds? First, it will be helpful to be clear about why you want to do this. Perhaps there's a job that pays more than you're currently making, but it requires heavy lifting, so you need to build strength so you can get the job—a practical reason with real-world implications. Similarly, you might have been clearing out the garage and realized you couldn't move some of the boxes—you recognize your limitations and want to finish the garage clean up or more generally to be able to accomplish tasks like this. Possibly you like to feel strong, enjoy a challenge, want to be a competitive athlete, or were inspired by someone else's physique. Your motivation could be that you feel some deficit, either in comparison to others or in contrast to how you would like to be. Maybe you're being bullied, and you want to build strength to defend yourself or to ward off future attacks. There are many possible reasons why you may want to strengthen your weight-lifting capacity, and it will be helpful to keep yours in mind as you advance in your training. In terms of dialogue, you want to keep in mind your motivations. You reflected on this in Chapter 1, so it may be helpful to review that section and make sure you're clear on what draws you to dialogue.

The next step in strength training is to assess your current capacity. How far are you from your goal? Are you pretty close? If you can lift 70 pounds, you already have a good foundation and don't have too far to go. But if you can only lift 30 pounds, it will take more time and effort to achieve your goal. In either case, your prior experience with weight lifting makes a difference. If you've done it before, you know how and can apply your prior skills. If you've never engaged in strength training, you will need to learn how to do it, and you will learn through experience what works for you and what doesn't. In terms of dialogue skills, where were you before you picked up this book? If the skills in this book were fairly new to you, you will likely need some practice in order to draw on the skills, especially in stressful situations. You'll need to be prepared for some possible setbacks and not get discouraged if it's difficult. On the other hand, if you're a mental health professional who has training in listening and in helping others manage emotions, some of the content is familiar, and you're simply applying it to a new situation. Even in this case, it may not feel effortless, as sometimes we have an easier time using these skills in professional settings than in our own lives.

Then there's the actual training itself. How will you prepare, and what support do you need? Do you own weights? Do you belong to a gym? Do you feel comfortable in the weight room, and do you know what to do? Do you need a trainer? Do you need a workout buddy? I was talking with a friend recently about strength training. I asked her if she used free weights or machines, and she said that because she doesn't feel comfortable in the weight room, she uses the machines even though she thinks free weights would be better. I used to feel this way, too, but when I was in graduate school, some of the other female students told me they were going to take a class at the gym called Women on Weights, and they invited me to join them. I had always felt intimidated in the weight room—there were very few women, mostly just grunting men—and I didn't know what I was doing. But then I took this class, and it took place in the weight room, so I got comfortable there, and the instructor taught us how to use the weights, so I knew what I was doing.

Does dialogue feel comfortable for you? It can be difficult if you feel unskilled and alienated. As you develop the skills, you may still be reluctant to enter into it if you and the people around you don't practice dialogue regularly. Sometimes it's easier when there are other people doing it with whom you feel like you have something in common, so you might want to seek out others who are similarly motivated to participate in dialogue. The Additional Resources that follow this chapter can point you in the direction of some organizations promoting and creating space for dialogue.

As with strength training, the more you work your dialogue muscles, the stronger they become. If you had never lifted weights before, and you tried to lift 80 pounds, it likely wouldn't go well. You might not succeed, and you would feel discouraged. Even worse, you might injure yourself and need to heal before you can even start training again. And if you have a bad outcome the first time you try it, you might give up on it altogether. The trick to success is to work your way to your goal slowly, learning proper form and strengthening the muscles little by little. It will also be helpful to have successes along the way by not pushing yourself too hard, too quickly. Same thing with dialogue skills. If you put yourself in a particularly challenging dialogue situation that doesn't go well, you might shy away from ever trying again. This is why starting with less charged interactions or topics may be a better way to start.

If you're someone who tends to jump into new experiences underprepared and then get discouraged, the incremental training metaphor may help you to slow down and build your dialogue muscles. If you're more likely to hold back and never attempt dialogue, it will still be helpful for you to build your muscles, but then you may need an additional push to actually use the skills.

Even with skills, people are sometimes reluctant to initiate dialogue. You've probably heard the Nike slogan "Just do it." I want to suggest a similar slogan for dialogue across political lines: "Just try it." You may not feel completely prepared, you may not feel like you can do all the skills precisely as I've described them, and you will certainly not know exactly how it will go. Don't let that stop you from trying to engage in dialogue. We are human beings, and there is not a perfect path.

If you're ready to try it, I encourage you to set yourself up for dialogue success by doing the following:

1. Keep your motivations in mind.
2. Assess your current strengths and consider what will be needed to build your skills.
3. Strengthen your skills, drawing on whatever supports you need.
4. Just try it.

Action Plan

Instructions: Answer the following questions to prepare for and plan to engage in dialogue. By reflecting on these questions, you can identify and seek out your own optimal conditions for engaging in dialogue across political lines. You may have considered some of these questions throughout the book; this will be an opportunity to clarify your current intentions.

1. Take a moment to review your original motivations for dialogue that you considered in Chapter 1. Are these still the reasons you want to have dialogue, or has anything changed? Maybe you've recognized the limits of persuasion and the potential for common ground? You might have gotten more curious about simply understanding others as a goal. Perhaps you've gained clarity regarding whom you want to dialogue with, and you've narrowed it down from a category of people to someone in your life. Write out your own motivation statement: I want to engage in dialogue across political lines because . . .

2. I feel confident in my ability to . . .
   - listen actively and nonjudgmentally (if not, review Chapter 3 and practice the skills in low-stakes situations).
   - manage my emotions (if not, review Chapter 4 and practice the skills in low-stakes situations).
   - understand others (if not, review Chapter 5 and practice the skills in low-stakes situations).
   - share my experiences and views (if not, review Chapter 6 and practice the skills in low-stakes situations).

3. I want to engage in dialogue with . . .
   - someone I know.
   - people who believe/value/do.
   - people I come into contact with.

4. I will initiate or be open to dialogue by . . .

5. The dialogue will take place at this time and location (if appropriate):

EXITING WITH INTENTION

You've learned how to initiate dialogue and how to engage in it, but how do you bring it to a close? You may want to end the conversation because you're out of time or because it feels complete. As mentioned in Chapter 4, there may be situations in which you feel unsafe or where you tried all of the strategies to manage your emotions, and you still want to end the conversation. Maybe you've realized that the other person is not in a space for dialogue. Perhaps, despite your best efforts, you can't calm yourself enough to listen and reflect. Possibly the conversation has been going for a while, and you're feeling depleted and want to continue at another time.

It's perfectly acceptable to bring dialogue to a close—to end it altogether or to pause and return later. When you're feeling distressed or depleted, it may be easier to close the dialogue if you've thought ahead about how to do so. When you are tired, triggered, or fed up, it is not the ideal time to craft your exit strategy. You may also find yourself more willing to enter a conversation if you feel like it's possible for you to end it gracefully.

When you're ready to bring the conversation to a close, you can express appreciation. Perhaps you will also share something you learned, a new insight you gained, or simply that you feel closer to them. If you want to continue dialogue at a later time, you can say so and invite the other person to another dialogue session, or you can end the conversation, knowing you can always reach out at a later time. If you're trying to exit quickly, ending a dialogue is most likely to go smoothly if you are clear and brief. Clarity is crucial so the other person understands that you are done with the conversation. Brevity will get you out of there fast. If there isn't a sense of urgency, if dialogue is coming to a more natural close, feel free to take your time.

Scripting Your Exit

You might consider these three components for an exit script, and I've offered some options for what you might say, as well as space to craft your own lines:

1. Appreciation
   a. Thank you for (your time, sharing your thoughts with me, _____).
   b. I appreciate (your honesty, your willingness to talk, _____).
   c. _____
2. Stating your intention to end the dialogue
   a. I'd like to end the conversation now.
   b. I'm not in the best place to continue this dialogue now.
   c. I think I've said what I need to say for now.
   d. _____
3. Indicating what you want to happen in the future
   a. I'm hoping we can continue talking at another time.
   b. I hope our differences don't stand in the way of our (friendship, working relationship, time together as a family).
   c. I wish you the best.
   d. _____

After the dialogue, it may be helpful to take some time to reflect on the experience, either individually or with someone else. Depending how emotional or perspective shifting the experience was, you might want to process it through expressive writing or debriefing with someone who can support you. I also invite you to share your dialogue experience with me. I am very interested in knowing how these conversations go—what worked, what was difficult, how the skills were helpful or not, your insights, questions, and feelings. If you would like to tell me about your dialogue, you can go to my website (http://taniaisrael.com/beyond-your-bubble).

KEVIN AND CELINE SAY GOODBYE

Let's see how Celine and Kevin bring their dialogue to a close.

Celine: Kevin, thanks for taking the time and effort to hear me out on these issues that have gotten us into trouble in the past. I feel like you heard me and where I'm coming from for the first time. (*Appreciation*)

Kevin: You're welcome. I gained a lot of insight from your openness in sharing with me and, really, from practicing these skills together. These issues are so painful and divisive that, in the past, listening felt counterintuitive. Practicing listening with you in dialogue has been eye-opening. I feel closer to you, even though we haven't come much closer together in our opinions. (*Insight and something gained*)

Celine: I feel like we're both passionate about our beliefs, and I can respect your passion, rather than take it personally or feel persecuted by you expressing your opinion. (*Insight and something gained*)

Kevin: Me too. I think I've gained some intellectual humility! (*Insight and something gained*)

Celine: I feel like it might be good for me to shift out of dialogue with you for now and try this with some other people. Do you think we can practice with our other family members now that we've survived each other? (*Intention to end*)

Kevin: I feel calmer and more effective about bridging some gaps now, yes. (*Something gained*)

Celine: There are a couple of people at the kids' school I'd like to try with, too. I feel like I can understand them a little better now, thanks to our practice, and don't have to give up my values to chat with them. (*Something gained*)

Kevin: I'd love to hear how it goes. And I hope you'll call me if there's ever a new issue you want to discuss, as you're thinking it through yourself. (*Future plans*)

Celine: I feel like we're fair representatives of opposing sides now. I invite you to do the same. (*Future plans*)

INTEGRITY AND GRACE

To engage in dialogue with someone across political lines, all you need to do is understand them and help them feel safe and understood. In this book, you've learned about and had opportunity to practice the skills that will help you get there: listening, managing emotions, perspective taking, and learning about them. You know that talking is optional, but when you do so, you should tell your story and be respectful and flexible. You've assessed your readiness, developed a plan, and prepared yourself for dialogue.

You have the knowledge and skills you need to move beyond your bubble. In addition to skills, my hope is that you will approach dialogue with integrity and grace.

Integrity

The word *integrity* comes from the Latin *integer*, meaning whole or complete.[1] Chapter 1 introduced the role awareness plays in intentional action. When our motives, reactions, and distortions are outside our awareness, it is difficult to be whole, to act in integrity. Dialogue can be most successful if we bring our whole awareness to it, and are alert to all of the knowledge of self, and others that is available to us, aligned with our intentions.

Yet integrity goes beyond the individual. It speaks also to strength of connection. When the construction of a building has integrity, it is safe shelter; when the weave of a fabric has integrity, it is difficult to tear apart. Dialogue will strengthen our families, friendships, community, and country. It will make us more difficult to tear apart. And that's a good thing.

Grace

Consultant and cartoonist Lisa Slavid reminds her audiences that "with relationship comes grace"[2]; if we're in trusting connection with one another, it's easier to be fallible and to forgive each other and ourselves for our failings. Intellectual humility helps us to be graceful, to be righteous without being self-righteous (Chapter 5). But it may not offer us grace, meaning forgiveness. Dialogue is difficult, and we need room to be flawed and to allow others to be flawed. We will aspire to do it well, but we will not always get it right. The more we strengthen our connections, the greater the integrity of our fabric, the greater our ability will be to seek and offer forgiveness.

THE POWER OF THESE SKILLS

We are being influenced by media, bots, and narratives crafted by political strategists. Psychology can be used to control us, or we can wield it to empower ourselves. You are now equipped with an understanding of psychological concepts and skills that enable you to move toward healing, connection, solutions. Dialogue is an opportunity to take back our power.

I want to leave you with a final thought. Even if you don't give a hoot about talking politics or finding solutions to societal problems, you will benefit from what you learned here. If we develop the skills that we need to have dialogue across political lines, we not only have a better chance at finding solutions to challenges we face as a society, these same skills will also help us to engage more effectively in our communities and schools and campuses. And these same skills will help us to be better coworkers, better partners, better parents, and better friends. Even if you don't care about any of that, these skills will help you feel better. They can decrease your stress and improve your well-being. The skills here are powerful tools. Go forth, and use them with integrity and grace.

NOTES

1. https://en.wikipedia.org/wiki/Integrity
2. Original credit to Jonathan Poullard and Felicia J. Lee of the Equity Consulting Group (https://equity-consulting.com).

ADDITIONAL RESOURCES

I hope that this book supports people who are seeking to engage in dialogue across political lines. In particular, *Beyond Your Bubble* is intended to help you build foundational skills that you can use in a variety of contexts and given a range of motivations for dialogue. So, this book is *a* resource, but it's not *the* resource—not the only thing that may be helpful to you. The sheer number of resources for dialogue that have surfaced since the 2016 U.S. election is some indication that you're not the only one who is interested in dialogue across political lines. People are using everything from books to podcasts to beer commercials to try to bridge the political divide. Here are some resources that may complement this book and provide you with opportunities to deepen and apply your skills.

BOOKS ABOUT DIALOGUE

A number of books have been written over the past few years focused on civil discourse or dialogue in the context of political polarization. In *Talking Across the Divide: How to Communicate With People You Disagree With and Maybe Even Change the*

World, author Justin Lee shares his experience and offers guidance about conversations across political lines, especially for the purpose of persuasion. *Politically Divided: A How-To Healing Workbook for Friends, Families, and Couples* by Mitch del Monico consists of activities that people can engage in to bridge the divide. Anastasia Kim and Alicia del Prado's *It's Time to Talk (and Listen)* focuses on conversations about race, class, sexuality, ability, and gender in the context of political polarization. Jeanne Safer's *I Love You, but I Hate Your Politics* focuses on political conflict in personal relationships. Other books address specific barriers to dialogue, such as the language we use to talk about politics[1] or intellectual and moral development.[2] *Peacebuilding Through Dialogue: Education, Human Transformation, and Conflict Resolution* by Peter N. Stearns contains essays that consider dialogue in various contexts, including teaching.

OPPORTUNITIES FOR DIALOGUE

There are a variety of efforts to bring people together for dialogue, community connection, and to reduce political polarization. The National Coalition for Dialogue & Deliberation (http://www.ncdd.org) is a network of resources that support conversations across divides. With more than 700 individuals and organizations in NCDD, the groundswell of interest in dialogue is apparent. Here are a few U.S.-based national programs:

- Better Angels (https://www.better-angels.org)
- Living Room Conversations (https://www.livingroom conversations.org)
- National Institute for Civil Discourse (https://www. revivecivility.org/conversations)

DIALOGUE AMONG ELECTED OFFICIALS

Elected officials are in a unique position—they have opportunities for dialogue across political lines, both with their peers and their constituents, although it may be difficult for them to do so out of the public eye and without criticism from their supporters. Nonetheless, there are efforts to work in a bipartisan fashion, such as the Problem Solvers Caucus,[3] which was founded in the U.S. House of Representatives in 2017. There are more localized initiatives as well, such as those of the San Luis Obispo County League of Women Voters to promote civil discourse in public meetings.[4]

COMMUNICATION

More general guidance on communication can be applied to dialogue across political lines. Many people find Marshall Rosenberg's approach to Nonviolent Communication[5] beneficial for resolving conflict and deepening connections with other people. Melanie Joy describes the role of shaming in toxic communication and identifies strategies for effective dialogue, especially as it relates to veganism.[6] There are numerous books about listening skills for children and adults that you can search for within your favorite brick-and-mortar or online bookstore.

NOTES

1. Herzfeld, T. (2018). *How to have a civil conversation in an increasingly uncivil and hostile environment.* Independently published.
2. Conroy, P. (2019). *Let's get civil—Healing our fractured body politic.* E-Booktime.
3. Problem Solvers Caucus. (2019). https://problemsolverscaucus-gottheimer.house.gov/frontpage

4. Kimball, S. E., & Humphreys, D. (2017). *How to adopt and promote civility and civil discourse.* http://lwvodc.org/files/civil_discourse_handbook_june_2017.compressed.pdf

5. Rosenberg, M. B. (2009). *What is nonviolent communication?* https://www.nonviolentcommunication.com

6. Joy, M. (2017). *Beyond beliefs: A guide to improving relationships and communication for vegans, vegetarians, and meat eaters.* Roundtree Press.

COMMUNICATION GUIDELINES

Respect
- Encourage your dialogue partner to share their perspective and experiences without interruption.
- Don't make assumptions about their motives.
- Treat people as if they are intelligent, moral, and well-intentioned.
- You can challenge an opinion without attacking the person who holds the opinion.
- Refer to people with their chosen labels.
- Ask questions from a place of curiosity rather than judgment.
- Don't pounce on opportunities to point out things that are inconsistent or incorrect.

Confidentiality
Agree on the level of confidentiality you want to maintain:
- Is it OK for others to know that you participated in this dialogue with this person?
- Can you share what you learned about people who hold a particular perspective without identifying the specific person?

- Is there anything about either of your background or experiences that you would like to be kept confidential?
- Would either of you prefer for your views to be shared in an attempt to promote understanding beyond the two of you in the dialogue?

Speak from your own experience
- Rather than speaking about groups of people, try to speak from your own experience.
- Own your feelings rather than framing your feelings as caused by someone else, such as "I feel angry when you ____," rather than, "You make me angry."

Managing discomfort
- Keep in mind that you can each choose what to share and when.
- At times you may notice discomfort, but don't allow it to stand in the way of sharing. Distinguish between discomfort that you can tolerate and red flags that indicate a high level of distress.
- Breathing or taking a break can help to regain equilibrium.

Other guidelines
- Are there any other guidelines that will help to create a positive dialogue experience for either one of you?

ACTIVITIES TO TRY WITH A PARTNER

Here are several activities that were quite popular in my dialogue workshops, and will help you to build skills for listening and perspective taking. If you want to try them, grab a timer and a willing partner.

A. PRACTICE REFLECTING

You might want to review the material on reflecting in Chapter 3 before you start. For this exercise, work in pairs. Find a partner and decide who will be X and who will be Y.

1. Set a timer for 2 minutes. X will talk about a dessert that they really like and explain why, and Y will practice nonverbal attending and reflection. So Y should let X talk, and Y will use eye contact and moderate head nods and minimal encouragers, such as "Mmmhmmm." After X has shared about the desserts they like and why they like them, Y will reflect back something that they heard.

2. When you're done, reset the timer for 2 minutes and switch roles, so Y talks about a dessert they really like and why, and X practices nonverbal attending and reflection.

3. Before wrapping up, spend a few minutes talking about what was easy and what was difficult about nonverbal attending and reflection.

Some notes on the Practice Reflecting exercise:

I typically recommend practicing with a relatively neutral topic, like desserts. This may sound silly, but everyone has an opinion on dessert, and although some people think desserts are an easy topic, what we learn from these conversations may help when we discuss more controversial topics. For example, you might be worried that the topic is too simple and that there wasn't much to say. If your partner says, "I like ice cream," where can you go with it from there? I still suggest sharing a reflection, and then use silence to offer some additional space that invites the speaker to share more. You might hear, "I usually eat it plain, but when no one's around, I like to put chocolate sauce and nuts on top."

For some people, the most difficult part of talking about desserts is staying quiet. Rather than jumping in and bonding over love of brownies, slowing down and remembering to reflect may be a challenge. You may think, "We're totally on the same page," and then be surprised when you get a little deeper and find out that person likes butterscotch pudding—but for completely different reasons than you. Maybe they have childhood association with it, and maybe you just like the taste of it. Or you find butterscotch pudding exotic because you never got it as a child. This dynamic can also occur when discussing politics. You may be enthusiastic to find common ground, so when you hear something that you can agree with, you want to ally with the speaker. Although accord can cultivate connection, it's still important to give uninterrupted speaking time to the other person and reflect even before agreement.

If you feel like talking about desserts is too easy, you might try to make it more complicated by being analytical. You think you need to say something more interesting that goes beyond what the speaker is saying, so you say something like, "Is apple pie a symbol of patriotism for you?" Don't go there. Just keep it simple.

Other people find discussing desserts challenging. When a dietitian friend of mine tried this, she said she felt the urge to educate her partner about desserts rather than reflect. This may also happen in political discussions in which you feel compelled to share information about the topic that the speaker may not be taking into account.

Reflecting can also help a speaker clarify their thinking. Sometimes when they hear their own words, they realize it's not capturing exactly how they feel. Your partner might say, "I like chocolate chip cookies," and you say, "You like chocolate chip cookies," and they respond, "Actually, peanut butter chocolate chip cookies are even better."

B. PRACTICE ASKING QUESTIONS

For this exercise, work in pairs. Find a partner and decide who will be A and who will be B. If you're with the same partner as the previous exercise, keep the same letter you had earlier.

1. Set a timer for 2 minutes.
2. B chooses a topic to talk about, something they don't particularly like and why. It could be a famous person or an activity or a type of media (movie or TV show or book or podcast or commercial) or something else.
3. As B talks, A practices nonverbal attending, reflecting, using eye contact, moderate head nods, and minimal encouragers ("Mmmhmmm").

4. After B has shared about their topic, A reflects something they heard, asks one open-ended question, and then listens while B responds.

5. Then, reset the timer for 2 minutes and switch roles.

Last, talk with each other about what was easy and what was difficult about each of the tools: nonverbal attending, reflection, and open-ended questions. Also, did you notice any differences talking and listening to a topic about dislikes versus likes?

C. PERSPECTIVE TAKING

The perspective-taking exercise in Chapter 5 is based on an interactive activity that I used in my workshops. It's designed for two people. If you would like to try it, here are the instructions:

1. Decide who will be Orange and who will be Green.

2. Choose an issue to focus on. You'll each have an opportunity to express your views about something you feel strongly about (e.g., abortion, climate change, immigration). It may be particularly helpful to choose something where you also have strong feelings about people who are on the "other side" of the issue. Take a moment to think of what you want to focus on before you continue.

3. You'll also each have an opportunity to listen to the other person's views. You may find yourself in alignment with what they're saying, or you may not agree, or you may even feel targeted by what they're saying. It's only your job to listen. You don't need to respond. This is an opportunity to practice staying calm (see Chapter 4).

4. Orange will choose an issue that they feel strongly about and vent about a person who believes in the opposing posi-

tion. Allow yourself to express as much anger, frustration, or confusion as you feel. Green will listen (use skills from Chapter 3).

5. Next, Orange, pretend you are the person on the other side. Try to imagine what they think and feel about people like you, and with just as much passion, vent from the opposition's perspective. Express yourself with as much anger, frustration, and confusion as they might feel about you. Green will continue to listen.

6. Now, Orange, you're back to being yourself. Try to come up with as many reasons as you can think of that someone might hold views on this issue that are different from your own. You might consider their experiences, values, or other things that would lead them to different conclusions on this issue. Share your ideas with Green. Then, Green will try to come up with three additional reasons.

7. Switch roles, so Green has a turn.

8. Green will choose an issue that they feel strongly about and vent about a person who believes in the opposing position. Allow yourself to express as much anger, frustration, or confusion as you feel. Orange will listen (use skills from Chapter 3).

9. Next, Green, pretend you are the person on the other side. Try to imagine what they think and feel about people like you, and with just as much passion, vent from the opposition's perspective. Express yourself with as much anger, frustration, and confusion as they might feel about you. Orange will continue to listen.

10. Now, Green, you're back to being yourself. Try to come up with as many reasons as you can think of that someone might hold views on this issue that are different from your own. You might consider their experiences, values, or other

things that would lead them to different conclusions on this issue. Share your ideas with Orange. Then, Orange will try to come up with three additional reasons.

11. Both Orange and Green: Consider how you felt about people on the other side of this issue before you did the activity, and reflect on how you feel about them now. Do you notice any new insights about them or any shift in your feelings toward them?

INDEX

ABOUT THE AUTHOR

Tania Israel, PhD, holds a doctorate in counseling psychology and is a professor at the University of California, Santa Barbara. Dr. Israel leads dialogue skill-building workshops to help people connect across political differences and teaches about helping skills, leadership, and community collaboration. She has also facilitated educational programs and difficult dialogues on a range of topics, including abortion, law enforcement, religion, and sexual orientation. She lives in Santa Barbara, California.

Visit http://www.taniaisrael.com and follow her on
Twitter @BYBdialogue
Facebook facebook.com/BeyondYourBubble/
LinkedIn linkedin.com/in/tania-israel